THE
THIRD TIME AROUND

Also by George Burns

LIVING IT UP

THE
THIRD TIME AROUND

G. P. Putnam's Sons
New York

Library of Congress Cataloging in Publication Data

Burns, George, 1896-
   The third time around.

   1. Burns, George, 1896- 2. Comedians—United
States—Biography. I. Title.
PN2287.B87A37   791′.092′4 [B]   79-15370
ISBN 0-399-12169-2

Designed by Bernard Schleifer
Printed in the United States of America

For Googie

CONTENTS

EVERY CHAPTER MUST HAVE A TITLE

THIS IS MY third book. Twenty-two years ago I wrote my first one, in 1975 I wrote another, and here I am writing this one. Altogether I've written three books, which isn't bad for a guy who never read one. Well, that's show business.

Now don't misunderstand me, I think reading is a marvelous pastime, and it certainly can be exciting. For instance, if you're a man, try going to bed tonight with a good book and a cute blonde. If the blonde can't read, there's always television. And you women go to bed tonight with a good book and Robert Redford. You'll have a terrific time; they say he's the greatest reader in Hollywood.

Anyway, I've learned that when you write a book the most important factor is the basic overall construction; in other words, a book should have a beginning, a middle, and an end. If you've got that, you don't have to worry about the dull stuff in-between. Let me give you an example: In my book the beginning is page 1, the middle is page 128, and the end is page 256—it's that simple. When you know what you're doing there's nothing to it.

When my publisher, Putnam's, asked me to write another

book I thought to myself, why not write a bestseller. In the first place, more people buy them, more people read them, you make more money, and it doesn't take any more time to write a bestseller than it does to write a book that nobody buys. Since that was settled my only problem was what kind of bestseller should I write? I made my own little survey and spoke to Dave Lefcowitz—he's my milkman. Here's what Dave came up with. He said, "You better ask somebody else." When you're in a spot you can always depend on Dave.

Anyway, I took his advice and talked to my friends at the Friars Club and Hillcrest Country Club and found out that among the most popular types of books today are cookbooks, travel books, historical novels, and adventure stories. Well, I decided that of those four categories the easiest one for me would be to write a cookbook. After all, I've been eating all my life. In fact, I don't know anybody who's been eating longer.

Now I realized there were all kinds of cookbooks on the market, so I came up with an idea that was different—a cookbook of simple thrifty recipes for people with very little money to spend. My first recipe was a soup that was my favorite when I was a little boy. My family was extremely poor, and my mother used to make this delicious soup that cost practically nothing. Just thinking about it made my mouth water, so I fixed myself a bowl. I got a pan of water, put in some ketchup, added some black pepper and salt, and let it come to a slow boil. Then I poured it into a bowl and tasted it . . . .

So I decided to write a travel book. I figured everybody likes to travel, so I picked out the most exotic place I could think of. Why not write a book about Tahiti? This time I was so sure I was right I didn't even bother to consult Dave Lefcowitz. I put on my writer's coat, the one with the brown suede patches on the elbows, lit up a pipeful of aromatic tobacco, got myself a pad of paper and a half dozen sharp pencils, and I was ready to write. Well, I sat there . . . and I sat there . . . and I sat there.

Finally I figured out what my problem was—I'd never been to Tahiti.

This might have stopped an ordinary writer, but not a fellow who was dressed up like I was. Actually the solution was simple. The shelves are full of books about Paris, Rome, Tokyo, Athens, London, Cairo, Madrid, Helsinki, but those towns have been kicked. We've got dozens of places right here in the United States I could write about, beautiful places that you've probably never been to. In fact, I'm thinking of a place right now that I know all of you would love, and I think you should go there—Ronkonkoma, Long Island. During my days of vaudeville I played Ronkonkoma at least three or four times, and every night after the show I'd head straight for the town's most exciting spot, White's Cafeteria. And what made it exciting was the cashier. She was a sexy, well-built little redhead who . . . who . . . who . . . who must be about eighty years old by now.

It was then I decided to write a historical novel. So again I sat there, but nothing happened. The only historical event I remember is Washington crossing the Delaware. The reason I remember it so well, halfway across the General said to me, "Will you stop singing and row faster" . . .

Then I thought I'd write an adventure story . . .

Maybe I'd write a mystery story . . .

Why not science fiction . . .

Anthropology? . . . No, not anthropology. I knew less about anthropology than I did about Tahiti. I'd never been to either one of those places.

I was so depressed I planned to give up the whole thing. I poured myself a cup of hot coffee, took off my writer's jacket, put out my pipe, and broke the points off my pencils. I was just about to tear up my pads when I glanced down, and there was that cup of coffee. That's when it came to me! I'll write a book about sex! Well, I'm at the stage now where the only thing that turns me on is a cup of hot coffee. What I couldn't figure out was why I didn't think of writing a book about sex in the first place. Sex is the Universal Language in which nobody speaks; they don't have to. As the well-known philosopher Dr. J. J. Cromwell once said, "Put an Eskimo man in bed with a Polynesian woman—" That's when he left the room, that's all he said. It so intrigued me I ran after him, but I was too late. He was going down the street on his skateboard.

When I made up my mind to write about sex I gave it a lot of thought and came to the conclusion that there's one thing that makes it so popular: You don't have to get dressed for it. Furthermore, writing about sex has become a very lucrative business. Look at Harold Robbins and Irving Wallace. Both of them made a fortune out of sex. The only one I know who made more is my sister Goldie. And sex should be a simple subject to write about. After all, it's been with us since time began, and always will be with us until somebody finds a substitute for it. Which incidentally I've been looking for for some time now. (If you readers hear of anything, please throw it my way.)

Anyway, once the decision was made to write about sex it was a great load off my mind. All I had to do was put it down on paper, and I figured I'd write a book of 250 or 300 pages. I knew I could do it, I had the paper.

I planned on starting the first thing in the morning, so I went to bed early and had a marvelous night's sleep. When I woke up the next morning I even had the title, *Sex Is a Many-Splendored Thing*! I jumped out of bed—well, didn't exactly jump, I made it out of bed—and opened the window. It was a gorgeous day. The sun was shining and the birds were singing—naturally, I harmonized with them. You know I love to sing. I did my deep breathing exercises, went into the bathroom, brushed my teeth, shaved, and stepped into a nice hot shower. As I was drying off I happened to glance at myself in the mirror. Then I took a look at myself in the mirror. Then I took a *lonnnnnng* look at myself in the mirror. That's when I decided to write about Tahiti again. My dreams of being another Harold Robbins or Irving Wallace were shattered. I put my robe on fast so I wouldn't get any more depressed than I was. I didn't know what to do, so I started combing my hair. It was lying there, so I figured why not comb it. I'd never felt so low in my life. This could be the end of my career as a writer.

Even breakfast didn't lift my spirits. Everything was tasteless. Over my second cup of coffee I got to thinking; whatever gave me the idea I could write a book about sex in the first place? Things are different today than when I was young. In those days a fellow would meet a girl, they'd keep company, they'd get engaged, they'd get married, they'd raise a family and stay that way. Today marriage is old-fashioned, it's like getting your spats cleaned. If a boy and girl like each other, they live together, have a couple of kids, and if they like the way the kids look, then they get married. And if the kids are ugly, the parents can always get a divorce, start living together, and be happy again.

Of course, things are different for me nowadays, too. When I was young, before I got married I had a very exciting sex life. In my neighborhood I was known as the "Romeo of Rivington Street." I had all kinds of girls. There was Big Rose Siegel, and there was Little Rose Siegel, and that's about it. Now I spend my evenings in a comfortable chair watching television and smoking a cigar. I found out that smoking a cigar is much easier for me than being a great lover. With a cigar I don't have to remember its birthday; I don't have to worry about meeting its mother; I don't have to take it out dancing; I don't have to get undressed to smoke a cigar; and when I'm through with a cigar I don't have to call a taxi to take it home. You want to know the truth, I've reached the point now where sex is a spectator sport.

Anyway, after struggling and knocking my brains out trying to figure out what kind of book to write I came to the obvious conclusion: Why not write a book about the subject I know best—me. I've known me for eighty-three years, and during that time I've become very well acquainted with myself. So that's what this book is going to be about, and as you read it I hope you learn to love me as much as I do.

With all humility, thank you,

G. B.

ME (WHO ELSE?)

To LOOK AT me now you might not believe it, but I was born. As I recall, it was at a very early age. Now most people can't remember back that far, but I must have a remarkable memory. I remember the very moment I was born. I made my entrance into the world singing. The doctor held me up by my heels and kept slapping me, but I wouldn't stop until I finished two choruses of "Red Rose Rag." Then when I started singing "My Gal Is a High-Toned Lady" he put me in the incubator and turned off the heat. If I hadn't been smoking a cigar, I might have frozen to death. This had a great effect on my life. To this day whenever anyone picks me up by the heels and starts slapping me I go right into "Red Rose Rag." It happened just last night during dinner. I'll never be able to eat at Chasen's again.

Well, everything you've read up to now is a lie, which proves what a truthful man I am. If I tell you something is a lie, you know it's the truth.

And now that you understand my character, let me tell you how it developed. I came from a very large family. There were seven sisters, five brothers, and no mother or father. We were so poor we couldn't afford parents. Look, I know that's an old joke, but I couldn't think of anything else. You're just going to have to get used to my writing style, I'm too old to change it.

I better start at the beginning. My father's name was Louis Phillip Birnbaum, and my mother's maiden name was Dorothy Bluth. They both came from Eastern Europe and their families knew each other even though they lived in different cities. My parents' marriage was prearranged practically from the day they were born, and it was the custom in those days that in a prearranged marriage the bride and groom didn't meet until the day of their marriage. When the day arrived my mother was fourteen and my father was sixteen. I understand my grandmother was very relieved, she was afraid my mother might become an old maid. Even though my mother and father had never met before, I guess they learned to like each other, because before they were through they had twelve of us. Can you imagine getting married at fourteen? When my son Ronnie was fourteen he was still selling hot hub caps. But he was a good boy, he not only sold them to me wholesale, but he gave me a professional discount because I was in show business.

When my parents got married, conditions in Eastern Europe were pretty grim, and it was everybody's dream to leave there and come to America. So two years and two children later my father arrived in New York City and began living with some friends on the lower East Side. And since they were all strangers in a strange country, they became a very close-knit community. My father was able to find a job working twelve hours a day in a sweatshop pressing pants. By scrimping and saving, and with the help of his friends, he finally had enough money to send for my mother and their two kids. It took them about two weeks to get here by steerage. I'm sure the only reason they came by steerage was that TWA was on strike at the time.

When they arrived my father had arranged for them to move in with another family, for which he paid the enormous sum of five dollars a month. I don't know whether the crowded conditions had anything to do with it, but the Birnbaum family started to grow. They already had Morris and Annie, and soon there was Isadore, and then Esther, Sarah, Sadie, Mamie, Goldie, Nathan (the author), Sammy, Theresa and Willy. My father should have been a watchmaker because the kids came like clockwork.

By the time Willy came along we had really come up in the world; we had our own apartment at 259 Rivington Street, four small rooms on the third floor of a tenement house. There was a coal-burning stove in the kitchen which was used for cooking and heating the rooms, and we had cold running water except in the winter when the pipes froze. If you had to go to the bathroom, you went down three flights and out into the yard where there were just three toilets for the whole building. Sometimes you had to wait five or ten minutes. But not me. I knew exactly when to come down so I never had to wait. That's where I learned my marvelous sense of timing.

We had gaslight but very little of it, because about once a week when the gas ran out you had to put a quarter in the meter. My mother always kept the flame turned down very low to make the quarter last as long as possible. In fact, the light was turned down so low I was eight years old before I knew what my sisters looked like. Then one night my mother turned up the light, I got a look at my sisters and blew it out. They were happy, too, because they weren't too hopped up about the way I looked either.

Our family entertainment was pretty limited. In those days there was no television or radio, and we certainly couldn't afford the movies. Our idea of a fun evening was to sit in the kitchen and look out the window at the neighbors' wash. Sometimes that wash was pretty exciting. One time my sister Mamie jumped up and said, "Look, Mrs. Mittleman got new bloomers!" And you could always tell when the Goldbergs on the fourth floor had a fight. Mrs. Goldberg would hang out the family wash, and then Mr. Goldberg had to hang out his own. Except on Wednesday. On Wednesday she'd hang his wash out first because that's the day he brought home a paycheck.

Thursday was bath day for us Birnbaum kids, and it was quite a project when you consider that we didn't have a bathtub. In fact, nobody in the whole neighborhood had a bathtub. Here's how the project worked. My mother would boil water on the kitchen stove and pour it into a washtub. And that one tub of water took care of all of us, because it was expensive to heat water. When the tub was full all the boys had to leave while the girls bathed. The oldest girl went first and the others followed in order. Believe me, nobody had time to play with a rubber duck. It was just into the tub and out, because we didn't want the water to get cold. Then the girls would dress as fast as they could and rush out and the boys would rush in. We moved around so fast we looked like a Mack Sennett comedy. We had to, that bath water was still cooling off. Like with the girls, the oldest boy went first. This routine was pretty tough on my youngest brother, Willy. By the time it was his turn he was dirtier when he got out of that water than when he went in.

You know, when I look back on those days on Rivington Street it makes me realize how lucky kids are today. They've got organized playgrounds, Little League, field trips, and in the summer they all get on buses and go to summer camps where they have swimming pools, basketball courts, baseball diamonds, and even a counselor to hand them a Kleenex in case they sneeze. When I was a kid we had none of those things. Our playground was the middle of Rivington Street. We only played games that needed very little equipment, games like kick-the-can, hopscotch, hide-and-go-seek, follow-the-leader. When we played baseball we used a broom handle and a rubber ball. A manhole cover was home plate, a fire hydrant was first base, second base was a lamp post, and Mr. Gitletz, who used to bring a kitchen chair down to sit and watch us play, he was third base. One time I slid into Mr. Gitletz; he caught the ball and tagged me out. There was no such thing as a uniform. One kid on the block showed up with a baseball cap and we made him go home. We didn't want to lose our amateur standing.

Our swimming pool was the East River. When we got tired of playing baseball we'd wave goodbye to Mr. Gitletz, run down to the river, take off our clothes, and jump in. This took a pretty strong stomach because the East River was full of garbage. When we'd swim we had to use what we called the "overhand slap" stroke. We'd slap the water with our right hand, and this would clear a path through the garbage. Then we'd slap it with our left hand, and that's the way it worked. I'm not sure, but I don't think Mark Spitz would have enjoyed this.

Using the overhand slap you could swim about five yards in five minutes. But there was one advantage. If you got tired, you could always crawl up on the garbage and rest. And if you were lucky, sometimes you'd find an apple with only one bite out of it.

After a refreshing swim we'd all get up on the garbage and walk back to the pier. Then we'd put on our clothes and head for home. After that swim, believe me, people knew we were coming three blocks before we got there.

The big treat for the little girls in the neighborhood was when Luigi the organ grinder came around with his monkey. Luigi was a big, good-natured Italian fellow, and the monkey's name was Toto. Toto wore a red velvet pillbox hat and a red velvet suit with gold buttons and a green sash. That monkey looked so good all us kids thought Luigi was working for him. Now seeing a monkey caused a lot of excitement on Rivington Street; the only animals we saw were stray cats and dogs running around. I remember bringing a dog home once, but he only stayed a couple of days. He left when he found out he had to take his bath after Willy.

When Luigi played the organ all the little girls started to dance. Everybody gathered around, and people stuck their heads out of windows and threw pennies which Toto tried to catch in his hat. For us kids this was more fun than watching Mrs. Mittleman's new bloomers. And it was my first taste of show business. When I saw that audience I jumped right in and started dancing along with the girls. We improvised all sorts of steps as we went along. We'd leap and twirl and do high kicks, and if I do say so myself, I was more graceful than most of the girls. My toes were always pointed, my back was arched, and my wrists were very loose. In fact, my mother was getting worried about me. When I recall times like that it makes me think that maybe kids today aren't so lucky. I'd give anything to hear Luigi play that organ again. But I don't think I'd get up and dance. My back is still arched, but now it's in the other direction.

There was never any problem finding somebody to play with because the streets were loaded with kids. And it's not hard to figure out why. In our building alone there were sixteen families, and each family had between eight and ten kids. When we were all playing together in the street there were so many of us we'd get mixed up and forget which family we belonged to. At nine o'clock in the evening my mother would holler out the window, "Come on up, children, it's time to go to bed!" We'd all rush up, and my mother would stand there with the door open. When the house was full she'd close it. Sometimes I made it, sometimes I slept in the hall.

In the summer I used to sleep on the roof under the clothesline. My favorite spot was right under Mr. Rosenbloom's underwear. I always opened up the flap so in the morning when the sun came up it would shine through on my face. I was the only kid in the neighborhood who had a suntan with but-tonholes in it.

That last part isn't true, but I was rolling so good I couldn't stop myself. Look, I may exaggerate now and then to try to be a little amusing, but basically this was the way we lived. We were poor, our neighbors were poor, we thought everybody in the world was poor. Our idea of somebody being rich was the Feingolds who lived on the corner. They had curtains in their windows. I remember I used to get up early in the morning and steal their garbage. Then I'd put it in our can. I wanted people to think we were doing well.

EVERY FAMILY SHOULD HAVE A MOTHER OR FATHER

To THIS DAY what amazes me is how my mother and father managed to raise twelve kids under the conditions we lived in. But whatever they did must have been right, because every one of us turned out fine. None of us wound up in jail, none of us were alcoholics, and none of us got mixed up with drugs. And there was a reason for this: We couldn't afford it. The only thing that turned us kids on was if there was a little meat in the gravy. Nobody made gravy like my mother. And it was a damned good thing because we had it seven days a week.

There was only one thing better than my mother's gravy and that was her coffee. Every morning one of us kids would go down to the grocery store, and for five cents we'd get a half gallon of milk. Now this was raw milk with no cream in it, so it was sort of a bluish color and very thin. My mother would pour this into a coffee pot and put it on the stove. Then she'd float some chicory on top, and when the milk came to a boil the chicory would sink to the bottom. This not only flavored the milk but changed the blue into a nice coffee color. Next she poured this through a strainer into our cups, and that was our morning coffee. If Maxwell House had tasted this coffee, they would have gone into some other business. In fact, on Rivington Street my mother was known as Mrs. Olson.

We were a very close family, and it wasn't just because of my mother's gravy and coffee. When you're twelve people living in four little rooms, you've got to be close. Now a highlight on the Birnbaum social calendar was when our relatives would come over and we'd all sit around and listen to my sister Sadie sing. Actually, Sadie hated to sing, and the rest of us kids hated to hear her, but my mother thought she had a beautiful voice. It was sheer torture for Sadie to stand up and sing in front of people, but when my mother said "Sing!" Sadie sang. So Sadie wouldn't be embarrassed my mother would allow her to go into the bedroom and leave the door open. Then standing in that dark bedroom Sadie would sing, and we'd all listen from the other room. I recall one night just as she was building up to her high note, my Uncle Frank got up and closed the bedroom door. I think that was the last time he was ever invited to one of our musicales. I'm sure you're wondering why my mother didn't ask me to sing; after all, that's what later made me famous. But you see, Sadie knew all the traditional Jewish folk songs and lullabys. All I knew was "Rufus Rastus Johnson Brown, Whatcha Gonna Do When De Rent Comes Roun'. " I sang that once for my Uncle Frank, but he was so religious I had to sing it with my hat on.

I think that one of the things that kept us kids pretty much in line was the respect we all had for our parents. It wasn't something that was forced on us; it was just there. It was natural, we were born that way. I never remember my mother slapping me, and I'm sure that went for my brothers and sisters. We may have deserved a good wallop once in a while, but that wasn't the way my mother operated. She was a very practical lady, and .she dealt with our problems with patience and understanding. Nothing ever seemed to fluster her.

A perfect example happened when I was seven years old. I was singing with three other Jewish kids from the neighborhood. We called ourselves the Peewee Quartet. Now there was a big department store, Siegel & Cooper, which threw an annual picnic, and the highlight was an amateur contest with talent representing all the churches in New York. Right around the corner from where we lived was a little Presbyterian church. How it got in that neighborhood I'll never know; it certainly didn't do big business. Well, they had no one to enter in the contest, so the minister asked us four kids to represent the church. We jumped at the chance. So that Sunday there we were, the Peewee Quartet—four Jewish boys sponsored by a Presbyterian church—and our opening song was "When Irish Eyes Are Smiling." We followed that with "Mother Machree" and won first prize. The church got a purple velvet altar cloth, and each of us kids got an Ingersoll watch which was worth about eighty-five cents.

Well, I was so excited I ran all the way home to tell my mother. When I got there she was on the roof hanging out the wash. I rushed up to her and said, "Mama, I don't want to be a Jew anymore!"

If this shocked her, she certainly didn't show it. She just looked at me and calmly said, "Do you mind me asking why?"

I said, "Well, I've been a Jew for seven years and never got anything. I was a Presbyterian for one day and I got a watch," and I held out my wrist and showed it to her. She glanced at it and said, "First help me hang up the wash, then you can be a Presbyterian." While I was hanging up the wash some water ran down my arm and got inside the watch. It stopped running, so I became a Jew again.

In situations where most mothers would have become very upset and excited, mine took it in stride. She had a way of solving a problem, and you didn't even know she was doing it. When I was seventeen I started running around with a girl named Jean DeFore who I thought was the greatest thing since ketchup. And you didn't have to hit her on the bottom to get her started. Jean DeFore was six years older than I was, and believe me, nobody would mistake her for Mary Poppins. At that time if a girl wore a little bit of rouge, she was considered fast and loose. Well, Jean not only used rouge, she wore beaded eyelashes and lipstick. And to top it all, she penciled in a black beauty mark on her cheek. All she needed was a red lantern hanging around her neck. If you're wondering why a seventeen-year-old kid would get mixed up with a girl like that, stop and think about it. It's better than playing with a rusty knife and cutting yourself.

When Jean had all- that makeup on she may have been twenty-three, but she looked more like thirty. But I was so proud that she'd go out with a seventeen-year-old kid that I couldn't wait to take her home to meet my mother. So one Sunday afternoon I did just that. As soon as we got in the door I said, "Mama, I want you to meet my sweetheart, Jean DeFore."

My mother was all smiles, not a hint that anything might be unusual. "Sit down, Jean," she said, indicating a chair. "Make yourself at home." Well, we all got comfortable, and in a very friendly manner my mother asked Jean if she were Jewish. Jean said she wasn't, and then my mother inquired, "Do you understand Jewish?" Again Jean said no. Turning to me and still smiling sweetly, my mother said in Jewish, "Is this lovely lady planning to adopt you?" Then looking directly at Jean, in a motherly tone she said, "I just told my son what a charming girl you are."

That's the way my mother operated. In a nice way she had made me realize how perfectly ridiculous I must have looked.

Where my mother was very realistic about things, my father was exactly the opposite. He was a dreamer. And being extremely religious he felt that life here on earth was just a stopover on our way to the hereafter. I didn't mind stopping over, but I thought it would be nice to have a little something in my stomach before continuing that trip. If I said my father was the worst provider in the world, I'd be lying. He wasn't that good. It wasn't that he didn't love us because he did very much, but trifles like food and rent and clothing never even crossed his mind.

There was an aura about my father. I don't know how to describe it, but there was something so impressive about him that with no particular effort he commanded love and respect. Not only his family, but the entire community looked up to him. He had long since given up his job as a pants presser and now spent most of his time at the synagogue reading religious books and discussing philosophy with other scholars. Occasionally he would bring a little money into the house which he earned as a *mashgiach*. Now being a *mashgiach* is not the kind of a job that's going to put one into a high-income tax bracket. You see, in an orthodox Jewish community if a family has an engagement party, a wedding or a bar mitzvah, they hire a *mashgiach* to make sure that everything is kosher. There was no set price for this service; the families paid what they could afford. Sometimes it was nothing. But when my father came home with nothing it didn't bother my mother; even when he got paid it was so close to nothing she could hardly tell the difference.

Being a *mashgiach* wasn't my father's only source of income. He was also a part-time cantor. And sometimes he'd sing at the services of one of the small synagogues. This didn't happen very often because his singing voice sounded a lot like mine. I remember one year he was asked to sing at a tiny synagogue on Clinton Street for the High Holidays. This was a very poor little synagogue, so my father agreed to do it for nothing. That night the period of fasting was over so all of us were gathered in the kitchen waiting for dinner. My father was laughing and joking and teasing us kids; he seemed unusually elated. My mother didn't exactly share his mood because she was busy trying to water down a stew to the point where it would feed a bunch of kids who hadn't eaten in twenty-four hours. She looked at my father and said, "What are you so happy about, that synagogue is paying you nothing." My father turned to her, and with a big broad smile said, "I know, but they asked me to come back again next year." Let's face it, my father was not handled by the William Morris Agency.

Although his religion was the most important thing in his life, my father did have a sense of humor. As I mentioned before, our house was always full of kids running in and out. Well, one night when my father came home and sat down in his favorite rocking chair, a little boy ran over to him and jumped into his lap. He held up the boy and said to my mother, "Dassah, which one is this?"

She turned from the stove and said, "Don't be silly, that's the Steiner's little boy."

"Thank goodness," my father sighed, "I've been gone all day, I thought maybe we had another one."

It's very difficult for me to write about my father, because my recollections of him are rather vague. I was only seven years old when he passed away, and he never allowed photographs of himself to be taken. He believed that having your picture taken was catering to your ego. But I do remember that he was a very gentle man, with kindly brown eyes and a long, full, impressive gray beard. That beard fascinated me. I used to pinch my face every day trying to make whiskers grow so I could have one just like it. And I don't think I ever saw my father unless he was wearing either his hat or his yarmulke. I often wondered if he took his hat off when he went to bed. Come to think of it, I guess he didn't have time.

My father never showed any favoritism to any of us children. He loved us all equally. My mother expressed her love the same way, so there was no such thing as a spoiled child in our family. When my mother told us to eat, we ate; when she told us to go to bed, we went; when she said it was time to go to school, we'd go. It was like being in the army, except for one thing. Our Commanding Officer kissed us good night.

The day my father died left a lasting impression me. Since I was only seven this was my first experience with death. I don't know what I expected, but I didn't realize it could be so quiet, so simple, and so sudden. It was a late Saturday afternoon, and my father was sitting in his rocking chair in the living room reading one of his religious books. My mother was looking out the window watching the kids dance to the organ grinder down in the street. I was on the floor playing. I heard my father call to my mother. "Dassah," he said, but she didn't hear him because of the music. "Mama," I said in a louder voice, "Papa's calling you." She looked around; his book had fallen to the floor and he was gone.

My father was only forty-seven years old when he left us, but as I said before he had the respect of the entire community, and his funeral certainly proved it. The whole Lower East Side turned out, and you couldn't move on Rivington Street. His death was almost more than my mother could cope with. She was only a child when she was married, so it was very difficult for her to imagine life without him. She had no choice but to continue her household duties, but every time the thought of my father being gone would come into her mind, she'd start to cry. We younger children didn't quite understand, but every time my mother cried, we cried. I don't know exactly how long this went on, but eventually life returned to normal and there were no more tears. However, my mother's tears may have stopped, but her thoughts of my father never did. Twenty-five years later after I'd married Gracie and was doing well, on one of my frequent visits home my mother and I had a cup of coffee, and she filled me in on the activities of the rest of the family. Just as I was about to leave she said to me, "Nattie, I want you to do me a favor."

I said, "Sure, Mama, anything you want."

"I think," she told me, "it's about time to put a new tombstone on your father's grave."

So the next day I took care of it. Up until then I didn't know tombstones wore out; I thought they lasted a lifetime.

I feel it's only right that I close this chapter with an observation. It's true that my father may not have provided me with too many material things, but he did give me a sense of responsibility, and he taught me the difference between right and wrong. For that I will always be grateful to him.

NEVER TRUST ANYONE WHO CAN'T SING HARMONY

As LONG AS I can remember I always loved to sing. It was something inside me that just had to come out. If you had something like that inside you, you'd want it out, too.

Even to this day my whole life revolves around singing. For example, as I write this we're having a water shortage in California, and in order to help out I make my singing work for me. When I'm taking a shower I sing a very fast song. That way I'm out in no time and save a lot of water. Of course, I do miss not going back for an encore.

Another way my singing comes in handy is with Arlette, my cook. She knows exactly what I want for breakfast by what song I sing. When I come downstairs if I'm singing "I'm Tying the Leaves So They Won't Fall Down," that means matzos, eggs, and onions. If I'm singing "When Uncle Joe Plays a Rag on His Old Banjo," that's bran flakes and bananas. But if I come down yodeling, that means only coffee this morning, I'm late.

I never stop singing. Even when I get in my car to go to work I sing to myself as I'm driving along. Of course, I always close the windows so nobody can hear me. If people are going to hear me sing, I want to get paid.

Now Hollywood is a big party town. You can go to a party practically every night of the week. And when celebrities are there it's a common thing for the host to ask them to get up and entertain. But when I give a party I don't put my guests in that spot. I bring in my piano player who can only play in my key and I never stop singing. It's amazing to me how many of my friends seem to be out of town whenever I throw a party.

I recall one time I planned a party for twenty people and eight people showed up. I guess the other twelve didn't like the dessert I always served. After dinner, as usual I got up and sang, and sang, and sang. I finally looked up, and the only ones left were Jack and Mary Benny. They had to stay, Jack was my best friend. By five after ten they were gone too. I guess you can only push a friendship so far. After they left I sang four more songs to Gracie. Of course, I had to sing them without music. . . . my piano player sneaked out when Jack and Mary left.

If I do say so myself, I'm a marvelous guest to have at a party. If things get a little dull, I jump right in and do two or three numbers. Sometimes I jump in before it gets dull. Once, Sylvia and Danny Kaye gave a party, and I went there with my piano player. Danny opened the door, let my piano player in, then closed it. Well, I figured Danny must not have recognized me, so I rang the bell. When he opened the door, I said, "Danny, it's me, George Burns." He said, "I know," and closed the door again. Well, I can take a hint, I don't have to have a brick building fall on me. I got in my car, closed the windows, and sang to myself all the way home.

Singing first became an important part of my life when three other kids and myself formed the Peewee Quartet. I was seven years old and sang tenor. A kid we called Toda was our lead singer. His right name was Moishe Friedman, so naturally we called him Toda. Our baritone was Mortzy Weinberger. We were all about the same age except Heshy Weinberger, who was eight. Heshy not only sang bass, but being older he was our business manager. If the Peewee Quartet were around today, I don't think the Osmond Brothers would lose any sleep.

It all started in the basement of Rosenzweig's candy store. After school the four of us each got five cents a day mixing the syrup that Rosenzweig put in his ice cream sodas. And as a fringe benefit we got all the sodas we could drink. By the end of the first week we could have opened a pimple factory. Toda's kid brother who was five years old tried to get a job working with us, but our manager, Heshy, threw him out. He told him he was too young to work.

There were four big copper vats, and our job was to pour in the extract of chocolate, vanilla, strawberry, and lemon. Then we'd stir it until it came to a boil, and bottle it. Well, when you stand there stirring syrup for two and a half hours a day for six days a week, it gets pretty monotonous. So as we were stirring we started singing, and before we knew it we were harmonizing with each other. And we didn't sound bad. Our favorite song was called "Dear Old Girl." Now "Dear Old Girl" was a very slow ballad, and naturally when you sing slow, you stir slow. When Rosenzweig heard us singing that song he'd run out on the street and holler down into the basement, "If you kids gotta sing, sing something fast like 'Row, Row, Row Your Boat,' I'm running out of syrups!"

The longer we sang together the better we sounded. Then one day we noticed that people were stopping at the head of the basement steps and listening to us. Well, when we saw we had an audience we stopped stirring altogether, stood in the doorway, and sang to them. We not only got applause, but they threw down a few pennies. At the end of the day we counted it up and we had made forty-two cents. Our manager, Heshy, was no dum-dum. He said, "Fellas, we made forty-two cents with our singing. That's over twice what we're getting from Rosenzweig." Our stirring days were over. We rushed upstairs, and Heshy announced, "Mr. Rosenzweig, we quit, we're going into show business!" Rosenzweig just stood there with his mouth open. He couldn't say a word. I guess he was stunned being in the presence of us celebrities. When we got out on the street we divided up the forty-two cents. Each of us got a dime, but Heshy kept the extra two cents because he was our manager. Besides, he was bigger than any of us.

That was the day I fell in love with show business. And here it is seventy-six years later and the romance is still going strong. I can still harmonize "Dear Old Girl," but please, don't offer me an ice cream soda.

We decided to call ourselves the Peewee Quartet. Of course, some people decided to call us other things. Anyway, our show business career started the next day. Right after school the four of us rushed down to the corner of Columbia and Houston Streets. We stood there and sang from three-thirty to six, and made exactly four cents. This meant a penny apiece, and there was no commission for Heshy. Mortzy took this pretty hard. "Fellows," he said, "I don't know about you, but I'm giving up show business. Tomorrow I'm going back to Rosenzweig's."

As we started back home we were all very discouraged until Heshy came up with a brilliant idea that saved the Peewee Quartet. He said, "Kids, we made a mistake. Instead of standing on street corners, tomorrow we'll start singing in backyards. That way people can't walk by us." And that's exactly what we did. The following day we hit about ten backyards, and by six o'clock we had made fifty-eight cents. However, we soon found out when you sang in backyards you had to be fast on your feet. Some people would throw down pennies, and sometimes you'd get a face full of dishwater.

By the end of the first week we were wet, but we each wound up with $1.30. There was no stopping us now. I don't know which one of us it was, but somebody came up with the idea that we could make even more money singing in saloons. It didn't matter that we were all too young to even be allowed inside. The first saloon we went into, Heshy walked right up to the bartender and announced, "We're the Peewee Quartet, and we'd like to sing for you and your customers."

The bartender shouted, "Get outta here!" and took a swipe at Heshy with a wet bar rag. But he missed him. Heshy was fast on his feet from dodging dishwater.

Back out on the street it was my turn to save the day. I said, "Fellas, we've made another mistake. The next saloon we go into we sneak under the swinging doors, and as soon as we get inside we start singing before they know we're there. If they like our singing, they'll let us stay." Everybody agreed, and we decided that when we finished singing Heshy would pass his hat around. It had to be Heshy because he had the only hat without a hole in it.

Well, at the next saloon we ducked under the door and went right into our opening song, which was "Goodbye, Girlie, and Remember Me." Sure enough, the bartender started to yell and went for his bar rag, but a customer stopped him. "The kids sound good, let 'em sing," he called out. We sang three songs, and when Heshy passed the hat everybody at the bar put something in it. And as we left, the bartender gave us each a baloney sandwich from the free lunch counter.

When we got outside the first thing we did was count the money. It came to sixty-five cents. Then Heshy went to take a bite of his baloney sandwich and a dime popped out of his mouth. Heshy was learning fast how to be a business manager. After that, first we looked in Heshy's mouth, then we counted the money.

Now don't get the idea that we scored in every saloon. Most of the time they threw us out. But that didn't bother us, we'd just move on to the next saloon.

However, it wasn't long before we wore out our welcome in every saloon on the Lower East Side. What we needed was a new audience, so we took the show on the road. We started singing on the Staten Island ferry. For a nickel apiece we could get on the ferry, and if we didn't get off, we could ride back and forth all day long. It worked out perfectly; every trip we had a captive audience. The only way they could get away from us was to jump overboard.

Now the Staten Island ferry had two decks, and the passengers would sit on benches. So whenever we would see a group of four or five people we'd stand in front of them and sing. Then Heshy would pass the hat, we'd check his mouth, and move on to the next group. We didn't do badly, but Sunday turned out to be our best day. On Sunday fellows would bring their girls with a basket lunch, and they'd spend the whole day riding the ferry. Well, we took advantage of this. Whenever we'd see a fellow begin to make love to his girl we'd jump in front of them and start to sing harmony. Of course, this would annoy the guy, so he'd give us a dime to sing on the upper deck. This trick kept us running up and down all day Sunday. We were making more money from people who didn't want to hear us sing than from people who did. But we finally had to give up playing the ferry boat, because most of the time we were only a trio. Mortzy Weinberger used to get seasick, and while the rest of us were doing our number Mortzy would be at the rail doing his.

Most kids would have been pretty discouraged by then. The ferry boats made Mortzy sick, the saloons had heard all our stuff, and the backyards meant a face full of dishwater. But that didn't stop the Peewee Quartet. We had a meeting and it was agreed that we should move into new territory. The following day was St. Patrick's Day, so we all put on something green and went up into the Irish neighborhood around Eighteenth Street and Tenth Avenue. All the saloons were jumping that day. The first one we went into we started right off with "MacNamara's Band," and we were a smash. We hit every saloon in the neighborhood, and by the time we were finished we had made over seventeen dollars, which to us was a fortune. We were standing on a street corner counting the money, when we looked up and there were ten tough-looking Irish kids coming down the street towards us. We didn't wait to find out if they were friendly or not, we just ran. And they took off after us. All we wanted to do was get back to our own neighborhood with that seventeen dollars. We must have run about two miles until we spotted this Jewish Boys' Club, and in we went. Inside there was a bunch of sixteen- and seventeen-year-old boys shooting pool, so we told them our problem. We explained that we had made over seventeen dollars and these Irish kids outside were trying to take it away from us. The biggest one in the group patted me on the head and said, "You boys are lucky you came here, we'll take care of this." With that they went outside with their pool cues and chased the Irish kids home. Then they came back inside, took our seventeen dollars, and chased us home. Well, that taught me a lesson that's still with me: Never go to a Jewish Boys' Club on St. Patrick's Day.

The Peewee Quartet hung together until I was about nine years old, and then we all went our separate ways. Mortzy and Heshy Weinberger became successful in the taxicab business. They both got married and raised grandchildren, and the last I heard they're retired and living in Florida. Moishe Friedman isn't called Toda anymore. He's now T. Harold Friedman and is a retired insurance broker living in a very nice house in Scarsdale. I'm the only one who didn't make good; I'm still in show business.

Those two years I spent singing with the Peewee Quartet must have been a great help to me throughout my entire career. As I mentioned before, I was a small-time vaudeville actor until I was twenty-seven years old. And when I say small, I mean the smallest. But I loved show business and never let anything discourage me. I was a singer, a dancer, a yodeling juggler, I did a rollerskating act, an act with a seal, I worked with a dog . . . you name it, and I did it. In those days if the manager of the theater didn't like your act, he'd cancel you after the first performance. I remember one Monday morning at the Farley

Theater in Brooklyn I was rehearsing my songs, and the manager heard the rehearsal and canceled me. I think it was the first time in show business that an act was closed before it opened.

But these things didn't faze me. I'd just think of the Peewee Quartet, and in comparison to a face full of dishwater or being hit with a wet bar rag, anything else was a step up. Anyway, I went from one cancellation to another until I met this little Irish girl, Gracie Allen, and we teamed up. Before long we started to play some good theaters, and people finally discovered I had a big talent. And I did—Gracie!

THE LOSING BREADWINNER

We were always a close family, but after my father died we became even closer. We all missed him not being there, but our family routine stayed pretty much the same. My mother had always been the one who handled everything. Although the three oldest children had married and moved away, there were still nine of us kids living at home. How my mother managed with practically no money coming in I'll never know. But she did. When Jesus fed four thousand people with seven loaves of bread and a few small fishes, he must have gotten the idea from my mother.

All of us kids did whatever we could to try to help out. Even though I was only seven, I decided to become the breadwinner of the family. I figured I'd been bumming around long enough, and it was time for me to go out into the world and seek my fortune. Of course, this was before I made my tremendous success with the Peewee Quartet. As it turned out, I wasn't exactly a breadwinner. I was more like the crumbwinner of the family.

Like most kids, every day after school I started out selling newspapers. Then I branched into all kinds of things. I became sort of a one-man conglomerate. And that was before I became a man, or before I knew what conglomerate meant. Newspapers in those days sold for a penny apiece. I'd start out with thirty-five papers and stand on the corner of Delancey Street and Clinton, which was a busy intersection. If I sold all the papers, I'd make seven cents. Sometimes I'd have eight or nine papers left over, and to get rid of them I'd run through the streets hollering things like "Extra! Extra! Ferry Boat Sinks in East River!!" or "Big Gun Battle in Sharkey's Restaurant!!" One day when I was stuck with eleven papers I took off down the street yelling, "Extra! Extra! Huber's Museum Goes Down in Flames!!!" Well, I was selling newspapers like hotcakes, when all of a sudden I felt a hand on my shoulder. It turned out to be a disgruntled customer. He held the paper in front of my face and said, "What are you pulling, kid? There's nothing in this newspaper about a fire at Huber's Museum!"

For a split second I didn't know what to say. Then I blurted out, "I know, that's such an early edition the fire hasn't started yet!" and ran.

I managed to save enough out of my newspaper earnings to branch out into the shoeshine business. I bought a can of polish for a nickel and got myself a little wooden box that I hung on a strap over my shoulder. I'd walk along the street selling shines for either two or three cents. For three cents I'd use a little polish, for two cents I'd just spit and rub. All I had was black polish, so if a customer had brown shoes, I'd sell him a newspaper.

One of my many big business ventures lasted exactly two hours and twenty minutes. I thought there was money to be made by selling vanilla crackers. I'd go into a grocery store and buy a bunch of vanilla crackers at ten for a penny. Then on the street I'd sell them eight for a penny. This meant that every time I sold eight crackers I'd make two crackers profit. The problem here was by the time I sold eight crackers I'd eaten two crackers. It didn't take me long to realize that this was the wrong business for a kid who was hooked on vanilla crackers.

Up to now my contributions to the Birnbaum Survival Fund hadn't been the greatest. But I figured if I kept trying sooner or later I'd strike it rich. I'd always heard that all wealthy men started at the bottom, and if this were true, I had a better start than anybody. For me to get to the bottom would be a step up.

When summer vacation came along I hit upon what I thought was my greatest idea. In summertime everybody needs ice, so why not go into the ice business. I made myself a pull-cart out of an apple crate and two old baby-buggy wheels. I nailed a stick on the front to pull it by, and I'd haul my cart down to an ice house by the East River and buy a hundred-pound cake of ice for five cents. Then I'd pull it back to my neighborhood, split the cake into four quarters, and sell each one for five cents. I was making a fifteen-cent profit on every cake of ice. By hustling I was able to do this three times a day, which meant I could make a profit of $2.25 in a five-day week. Unfortunately, I never made it to the end of the first week. In order to get to the ice house I had to go right through the middle of this Italian neighborhood, and on the fourth day I was happily running along with my second cake of ice when these two rough-looking kids stopped me. Right away I knew I was in trouble when one of them said, "Hey, kid, I never saw you in this neighborhood! What's your name?"

I knew I had to think fast, my ice was melting, and so was I. I had to come up with an Italian name, so I blurted out the only one I could think of, "Enrico Caruso!"

The biggest of the two stuck his face right in front of mine and snarled, "Are you Catholic?" I looked right back at him and said, "Are you kidding, my father's a priest!"

That was the end of my ice business. They took my cart and my ice and chased me all the way back to Rivington Street.

Well, this was the low point in my life. Here I was seven

years old and I'd already failed in four different enterprises. There was only one avenue left for me to take—I turned to a life of crime! And in a big way. I started stealing seltzer bottles.

I know this may shock some of you readers, but when my publisher asked me to write this book I promised to tell it just like it was. Of course, this confession might destroy my image as an ancient Casanova, but what the hell—that's a chance us sex symbols have to take.

Let me tell you how this little ripoff of mine worked. In those days people used to buy seltzer water in bottles that had a heavy lead top, and before they returned the empty bottles to the store to get a two-cent refund they kept them out on the fire escape. Now the first step in this caper of mine was to get my hands on those bottles. This involved going up on the roof, lowering a string with a hook on the end of it, catching it on the handle of the seltzer bottle and pulling it up. I got quite good at it. If I worked fast, within a half hour I could probably pull up twenty or thirty seltzer bottles.

I suppose you think the next step would be to take those bottles back to the store for the two-cent refund. Not me. I wasn't the Willie Sutton of my day for nothing. When I got about ten bottles I'd take them down to the basement, unscrew the tops, melt them and sell the lead for a much bigger profit. It worked out so that instead of two cents I got six cents for each seltzer bottle top.

Once I got the plan worked out I couldn't wait to put it into operation. The next day I played hooky from school. With all the money I planned to make I thought who needs an education? Looking back, it's amazing to me how stupid a kid could get in only seven years.

Well, the next morning there I was on the roof pulling up seltzer bottles. Within twenty minutes I had ten bottles. This was working out even better than I planned. Ten bottle tops at six cents apiece, there was forty-eight cents right there. (You can see what playing hooky did to my arithmetic!) I was gathering up the bottles to take them down to the basement when I got the feeling I was not alone. I looked around and there stood my mother with her arms folded, staring down at me. For a few seconds there was complete silence. Finally, with a weak smile, I said, "Mama, I'm not in the ice business anymore."

More silence.

I said, "Mama, I'm now in the used bottle top business."

"I can see that," she said, without changing her expression, "with other people's bottles."

"Mama, are you mad at me?"

"No, I came up here to take a tap dancing lesson!"

"But how did you know I was up here on the roof?"

"Everybody in the building knows you're up here. How often do people see seltzer bottles flying past their windows?"

Trying to plead my case, I said, "But, Mama, I was just trying to make money for us. I could unscrew the heads of these bottles and sell them for six cents apiece."

This did not impress my mother. "If somebody unscrewed your head, I don't think it would even sell for two cents," she said. "You're going to return every one of those bottles to the people you took them from!"

I couldn't stand the thought of facing all our neighbors. "Mama," I cried, "I can't do that."

"Yes you can, and I'll show you how! How many bottles did you steal from Mrs. Mittleman on the fourth floor?"

"Three," I whimpered.

Then pointing, she said firmly, "Pick up three of those bottles and come with me."

I felt like a drowning man going down for the third time. As I picked up the bottles all of my seven years flashed in front of my eyes. Like a whipped puppy I followed her downstairs and waited while she knocked on Mrs. Mittleman's door. When the door opened my mother gestured toward me, and with exaggerated sweetness, said, "Mrs. Mittleman, I'd like you to meet my son, the criminal."

I just stood there with my arms full of evidence and kept staring at the floor. "Now you march over to that window," my mother continued, "and put Mrs. Mittleman's bottles back on her fire escape."

Well, I rushed to the window, put down the bottles and got out of there as fast as I could. When we were alone in the hall, my mother said, "Up on the roof you said you couldn't return those bottles. Well, now I've showed you how. So you get busy and return every one of them right now!"

That's one morning I'll never forget. Not only had I been thoroughly humiliated, but here I was seven years old and all washed up. How could I go into another business with a criminal record? One thing this little episode taught me was that crime doesn't pay—at least, not like it does nowadays.

MARRIAGES ARE NOT ALWAYS MADE IN HEAVEN

HAVE YOU NOTICED that marriage seems to be on the way out? Well, I have. Maybe you've been so interested in reading this book that you haven't noticed it, but it's happening. People are just not bothering with the tradition of marriage anymore. Nowadays when a young couple meet, if he's got a rear seat on his motorcycle, they start living together. And after they start living together if some night the girl doesn't feel sexy, she can't use that old excuse about having a headache. When you've been riding around on a motorcycle all day it isn't your head that aches.

But I'm not criticizing the way young people do things today, I don't know whether it's good or bad. However, there's one thing I'm sure of, it's fast. When I was young, a couple had to be formally introduced. Now a guy sees a girl, he says, "Hiya, Foxy," and she says, "Your place or mine?" What's their hurry? Sex has been around for a long time. You may not believe this, but it was around before I was.

With all due respect to the kids of today, I think my generation had more fun. We made it last longer. Once a fellow met a girl he'd start going out with her, and maybe on the fifth date he'd steal a little kiss. After eight or nine months of keeping company they'd decide to get married, and the fellow would go to the girl's father and ask for her hand in marriage. Well, it's not that way today. Why should a fellow ask a girl's father for her hand? What does he want with her hand, he's already had everything else.

Our whole attitude toward living today is speed. Everything has to be done right now. Look around you. There's instant coffee, instant tea, instant soup, frozen dinners, take-out chicken, take-out pizza . . . it goes on and on. Anything you want, you can have in a matter of minutes. Now I think this was all brought about for the benefit of the younger generation. They want to get all that dull stuff out of the way so they'll have more time to do what they do best. And if you think what they do best is playing backgammon, you must still be wearing high-button shoes. The young people never quit. Even when they have leisure time what do they do? They go to a drive-in movie. You know, there's a fellow out in North Hollywood who owns a drive-in movie and he's making a fortune. Every night the place is packed and he doesn't even show pictures.

That kind of pace is not for me, and it never was. All my life I've taken things nice and slow and easy. And it paid off. I'm eighty-three years old and if I want some excitement, I get myself a bowl of hot soup. Come to think of it, maybe my pace was a little too slow.

In the neighborhood where I grew up none of the mothers would let their young daughters out after dark. Personally, I thought it was a mistake. If you could have seen some of those girls, they would have had a better chance getting a fellow in the dark. Actually it didn't matter when they went out because when it came to marriage, most of the girls had nothing to say about it. It was all handled by what was called a matchmaker. If a family had a marriageable daughter, they would send for him. He'd look the girl over, and for a fee he'd try to find an eligible young man to marry her. His fee would vary according to how much he thought the family could afford. For fifteen dollars he'd just go out and grab the first fellow he saw; for twenty-five dollars he'd try to find a guy who had his own store; at seventy-five dollars he'd go for a fellow who was studying to be a doctor or a lawyer; and if you could afford a hundred dollars, he'd divorce his wife and marry the girl himself.

Well, at those prices my family couldn't afford anything like that. After all, there were seven girls to unload, so my mother had to become her own matchmaker. The system she developed was uncanny. I don't know how she did it, but when anybody in the neighborhood had a young nephew or cousin, or any relative, close or distant, coming over from Europe, it seemed that she knew about it before they did. The day he arrived she was there to help him unpack, and that night he'd be having dinner at our house. All us younger kids were always very happy when it came time for one of our older sisters to be peddled. My mother made sure that we had an extra good meal that night to impress the prospective victim. The rest of the week we might be eating ketchup soup, but on that night we had chicken.

The seating arrangement at the table was an important part of my mother's strategy. She always made sure that the young man sat in the chair furthest from the door. That was in case when he got a good look at this group he'd try to escape. The only way this poor kid could have gotten out of that room would have been to dive through the fourth story window.

After dinner the rest of us would stay at the table in the kitchen with the door closed while my mother took the young couple into the front room to get acquainted. She'd seat the two of them on the couch, and then she'd sit in a chair and begin her pitch. She didn't waste any time; she got right to the point. This guy's still punchy from the boat trip he'd just made, and here's my mother reeling off my sister's great qualifications as a wife: what a great cook she is, how she sews all her own clothes, a marvelous housekeeper, lovable disposition, extremely religious, and most important of all, ending up by assuring him she's as pure as the new-driven snow. My sister is listening to all this wondering who my mother is talking about. My mother never bothered to ask the fellow what his plans were. All she cared about was that he was single, breathing, and Jewish.

I have to admit it didn't happen exactly that way, but look, I'm a member of the Friars Club, so I try to make it amusing. But whether it's amusing or not, my mother's system worked. My seven sisters all got married, raised lovely families, and none of them was ever divorced.

But there was one close call. My mother had arranged what she thought was a perfect marriage between my sister Mamie and a young dental student named Max Salis. Everything went fine while Max was struggling to get his diploma. But when he finally got it and hung out his shingle, for two months absolutely nothing happened. Max had gone deeply into debt for dental equipment and office furnishings, and even though he and Mamie lived in a small apartment in back of the office, there was no money coming in. One day Mamie came to my mother in tears. She was extremely upset. If Max didn't get some patients soon, it could possibly ruin their marriage. With no patients coming in, by the end of the day he was in such a state of depression he was impossible to live with. He considered himself a failure, and Mamie didn't know how to cope with it.

Well, as usual the next day my mother came up with a solution. Her idea was to have all us younger kids still living at home sit in the waiting room of Max's office. His windows faced right onto the street, and she reasoned that people passing by would look in, see the crowded waiting room, and figure that Max must be a fine dentist. Max didn't have much hope for the success of this idea, but he was so low he was ready to try anything.

For three days I sat there with my sister Theresa and my brothers Sammy and Willy. Nothing happened. Just when we were about ready to give up the whole idea as a failure, a woman started up the steps to the office with her little boy. I raced into the inner office and said excitedly, "Uncle Max! A patient is coming!" I waited a few seconds until I was sure the woman was inside, then I opened the door and came out into the waiting room, saying in a loud voice, "Dr. Salis, you're the greatest dentist in the whole world. I never felt a thing!" And with that I left. After making that dramatic speech I knew it would be only a matter of seventy-three years before I would win the Academy Award.

Well, from then on Max started doing business. In fact, things got so good that one day he came to my mother and said, "Please, would you keep your kids out of the waiting room, there's no room for my patients." Max was happy, Mamie was happy, and my mother had done it again. But I've got a little secret for you. Whenever I got a toothache I didn't trust Max; I went to another dentist.

By the time my two younger sisters were ready to get married they didn't need my mother. Things had changed, and girls were finding their own fellows. When my sister Goldie first started keeping company, it was with a young fellow named Willie Schusterman. When he'd bring her home after a date, they'd stand in the downstairs hallway and do a little spooning. They were standing right under the hall light, but they were so wrapped up in each other they didn't even notice the neighbors in the building who kept coming in and out. Well, my mother knew what was going on, so one night she went out and hollered down the stairs, "Goldie, why don't you bring Willie upstairs and kiss him in the parlor! All the neighbors have been watching you, why shouldn't I have a look?!" Anyway, it wasn't long before Goldie became Mrs. Willie Schusterman. And Willie was considered quite a catch. He owned a little store in Newark, and all he sold was straw hats. Actually, Willie was quite prosperous; that is, in the summer he was prosperous. In the winter he and Goldie had to eat the hats he couldn't sell in the summer.

Next came my youngest sister Theresa. She married a

fellow named Charlie Kalender who was a window dresser in Leopold's Haberdashery on Second Avenue. Now, that romance didn't blossom overnight. At that time Theresa had a job as a salesgirl in Klein's Department Store, and on her way home she always passed Leopold's. When Charlie would be working in the window and Theresa passed by, he'd wave to her and she'd wave back. This went on for about three months, and although Theresa liked Charlie's looks, nothing further happened. Theresa was getting desperate, so one evening as she passed the store and Charlie waved, she held a note up to the window which read, "How about a date?" Old Charlie picked up on this subtle hint in a flash. He held up a note that read, "I thought you'd never ask me." That night they had their first date, and a month later they were married.

This marriage worked out great for me. I was still trying to make it in show business, and every once in a while Charlie would bring me a suit that had been on display in one of the windows at Leopold's. However, being on display in the sun for so long the suit was always faded in the front. I remember one suit I had was dark brown in the back and gray in the front. I looked much better going away from you than coming toward you. From the side I looked like two people bumping into each other.

You'll notice that I haven't mentioned my brothers getting married. And there's a reason for it. My mother didn't have time to bother with us boys; she had a full-time job just getting rid of all those girls. But even though my mother wasn't directly involved as a matchmaker with my brothers and me, none of us would think of getting married before my mother met the girl and gave her approval.

Let me tell you how it worked with my marriage to Gracie. The first time my mother met her was when we were playing the Green Point Theater in Brooklyn. My mother saw the show and afterwards she came backstage to meet Gracie.

Now before I go any further, there's something I should

explain about our act. Gracie was absolutely marvelous on the stage, and I was just the opposite. The act was called Burns and Allen, but it should have been Gracie Allen and What's-His-Name. But as a straight man I did have a few lines. One was, "Gracie, how's your brother?" Another was, "No kidding, Gracie, what happened next?" And of course, there was, "Oh yeah?" There were others, but they were unimportant. For the finish of the act Gracie did an Irish jig and I tapped my toe and pointed to her feet. Then she'd exit by walking off the stage and I'd follow her. And believe it or not, I had the nerve to call the act George Burns and Gracie Allen.

But in spite of me the act was a hit, and after I introduced my mother to Gracie, she said, "Gracie, you're a very talented girl, and I can't tell you how much I enjoyed watching you."

"Well, thank you, Mrs. Birnbaum," Gracie said, "but what did you think of your son?"

"The people just laughed at everything you said," my mother answered, "and that little dance you did at the end was so darling."

"Well thank you, Mrs. Birnbaum, but what did you think of your son?" Gracie persisted.

My mother said, "He's a nice boy."

And that about summed it up, because that was one of the nights when Gracie made her exit and I forgot to follow her.

After that my mother met Gracie many times, and when we decided to get married, naturally I went to my mother to tell her. I said, "Mama, Gracie and I are going to get married."

A happy smile came over her face, and she said, "Nattie, you're a very fortunate boy. Gracie's a charming young lady. She's beautiful and talented, and I'm sure she'll make you a wonderful wife."

"But, Mama," I said, "I think you oughta know, she's not Jewish, she's Catholic"

She looked up at me and replied, "Nattie, if they'll have you, that's fine."

I once asked Gracie what her mother said when she told her she was going to marry me, and that I was Jewish. Gracie told me her mother said, "Maybe he'll get over it!"

Well, that's the way people got married when I was young. As I said at the beginning of the chapter, things are a lot different nowadays. And since I always like to keep right up with the times, I'm thinking of buying myself a motorcycle and a black leather jacket, renting a pad with a water bed in Laurel Canyon, and cruising the discotheques. But now I'm going to lie down. I got tired just thinking about it.

ALL MY BROTHERS WERE BOYS

Now I've told quite a bit about my sisters, so in all fairness I think I should give equal billing to my brothers. In order of appearance they were: Morris, Isadore, Sammy, and Willy. I made my entrance between Isadore and Sammy. None of us kids had a middle name. We were lucky we had any name at all. By the time my mother got around to naming one, there was another on the way.

I'm going to give you a little rundown on each of them, and since Morris was the oldest, I'll start with him. He was quite a bit older than I was, and my earliest recollection of him was after he had left home and would pay us occasional visits. He always dressed in very expensive clothes, and to look at him one would think he was the president of a corporation. Actually, Morris was a gambler, and like most gamblers he was either riding high or wondering where his next buck was coming from. But high or low, good or bad, he still managed to look like his corporation had just declared a dividend.

I'll never forget when I was a small boy, and Morris dropped by in one of his flamboyant moods. He breezed into the kitchen with a beautifully wrapped package, which he handed to my mother. All of us kids were very excited and gathered around the table while she unwrapped it. When she finished, all of us kids looked at her, she looked at us, and then we all turned and looked at Morris.

"Morris, what is it?" my mother asked.

Excitedly Morris said, "Mama, that's Russian caviar! That two-pound jar cost a fortune!"

This was exactly what we needed. We were then on the third day of a batch of my mother's potato soup, and Morris shows up with caviar. My mother just stared at him for a couple of seconds in disbelief, then, "Morris, I imagine for what you paid for this I could buy twelve pairs of shoes."

"But, Mama," Morris protested, "caviar is a special delicacy. You put it on a cracker and eat it!"

My mother said, "Good, we'll all eat caviar barefooted and without the cracker."

With that Morris opened the jar and asked her to taste it. She took a little, and then screwing up her face said, "Morris, you should return this and get your money back, it's spoiled. Look, it's already turned black."

I suppose you should be able to gather from this little incident that being practical was not one of Morris's strong points. If you're not already convinced, here's a beauty. Morris once got a crush on a little girl, and one night he decided to take a taxi to go visit her. Now this doesn't sound like such a big deal until you consider that Morris was in New York and the girl lived in Boston. I don't know what the taxi fare was, but a minor detail like that wouldn't bother Morris.

Those were things he did when he was riding high. But there was another side to the coin.

Years later when Gracie and I were doing well we were living at the Edison Hotel in New York and one night we got a visit from Morris. When he arrived Gracie was in the other room getting dressed to go out to dinner, and after the usual small talk Morris finally got down to the real reason for him being there. It seemed that he was a little short of cash, and he borrowed fifty dollars from me. When Gracie came in I invited Morris to have dinner with us. He said, "If you haven't made any plans, I know the perfect place—a restaurant on Second Avenue called The Little Gypsy, and they serve marvelous Romanian food." He went on to say how wonderful the atmosphere was, that they had the greatest zither player in the world, and a Romanian girl who sang beautiful gypsy songs.

This all sounded fine to us, so off we went. And it turned out to be everything Morris had said it was. We had a delightful evening. When we were ready to leave I asked for the check, and when the waiter brought it, Morris said in very impressive tones, "I'm paying that check," and he handed the waiter the fifty-dollar bill. Then continuing in grand style he instructed him, "Give ten dollars to the singer, ten dollars to the zither player, pay the bill and keep the rest for yourself."

Gracie was very impressed with Morris. Of course, she didn't know it was my fifty. On our way out while Gracie stopped in the ladies' room Morris turned to me and said, "George, I'm a little short, could you let me have fifty dollars?"

As I removed another bill from my wallet I said, "Why don't I give this directly to the waiter."

Morris took the fifty out of my hand, folded it, and put it into his pocket, saying, "Let's not spoil him, George."

I really owe a debt of gratitude to my brother Morris. Many of his close friends were actors in the Jewish theater, so Morris loved show business. He was the only one in my family who encouraged me to stay in it. And in my early days it wasn't easy for me to stay in show business, because everybody who saw me on the stage wanted me to get off.

Next in line came my brother Isadore H. Birnbaum. I know I told you that none of us had a middle name, but when Izzie started doing well he added the H. I once asked him what the H. stood for, and he replied, "It stands for H."

Izzie was the solid, industrious one of the family. He started out as a traveling salesman selling ladies' dresses, and he must have done a hell of a job because by the time he was twenty-eight he owned a department store in Akron, Ohio. All Izzie thought about was making a success out of his business, and he worked at it day and night. Come to think of it, he must have taken a couple of nights off because he and his wife, Madge, had two beautiful children.

Izzie always worried about me. All I could think about was getting into show business, and to him show business was the bottom of the barrel. He kept trying to convince me that I had no future as a performer and would only wind up as a bum. He didn't make much of an impression on me, because what he couldn't understand was I'd be very happy being a bum if I could do it with makeup on.

Anyway, when he started doing well in Akron, during one of his business trips to New York, Izzie came by the house. He sat me down on the couch in the living room and told me it was time we had a serious talk. I figured here comes the bum routine again, but this time Izzie had a plan for me. "George," he said, "you're sixteen years old and it's time we gave serious thought to your future. To begin with, you've had no education, so I've arranged for you to attend the Manhattan Preparatory School." He let that sink in, then continued with, "After four months there you'll come to my store in Akron and start out as an elevator boy. Eventually you'll work your way up, and who knows—someday you might even be a buyer in my store. You could make as much as seventy . . . eighty . . . maybe even ninety dollars a week!"

And there it was. However, if he expected that speech of his to make me give up my show business career, he was wrong. I said, "But, Izzie, I just read in the paper there's a young girl named Blossom Seeley in a Broadway show who sings 'Toddling the Tooddloo'—and they pay her a thousand dollars a week!"

He looked directly at me and said, "I've never heard Blossom Seeley sing, but I've heard you. And my advice to you is that you toddle that little toddle of yours down to the Manhattan Preparatory School early Monday morning."

Well, I lasted in that school exactly four days. The only thing I remember from this episode was that my teacher was a fellow named Leon Trotsky. I believe he eventually opened very big in Russia and later was canceled in Mexico. In case you're worried that I was influenced by Leon Trotsky, I wasn't. He never sang any of my songs, and I never used any of his philosophy.

Anyway, I never made it to that elevator in Akron. But years later when Gracie and I were successful we were headlining the Colonial Theater in Akron, and one night we had dinner with Izzie and Madge. I said to him, "Izzie, is that elevator job still open?"

He leaned over toward me and said, "George, let me tell you something. If it wasn't for me, you might never have made it in show business."

I didn't know what he was getting at, so I asked, "Izzie, what are you getting at?"

And very seriously he said, "If I had offered you a better job than running an elevator, you might have taken it." But he was wrong. I wouldn't have taken it if he had offered me the entire store.

Izzie was a wonderful man. He was a devoted husband and father all his life, and I can truthfully say that I never met a man as honest as my brother Izzie. If it's true that George Washington became president because he never told a lie, then Isadore H. Birnbaum should have been president. Well, maybe he told one little lie. Look . . . Secretary of State isn't a bad job, either.

After Izzie I was the next boy in the family. My parents had decided that I would be their last child, but after taking a look at me, my mother said to my father, "We'd better try it again, maybe this time we'll get it right." So along came my sister Theresa and then my brother Sammy.

Sammy was quite a character even when he was a kid. When he was about eight years old he decided he wanted to be a detective. And who knows, he might have become one if it hadn't been for one little unfortunate incident. He was caught in a five-and-ten-cent store stealing a detective kit. That night after my mother got through paddling his backside, "the detective" had to eat his dinner standing up. He didn't have to stand too long; we had very little to eat.

When Sammy was about seventeen he got a job with the post office and was making the princely sum of fifteen dollars a week. Out of this he gave my mother thirteen dollars and kept two dollars for himself. Even though he wasn't making much money Sammy always looked absolutely elegant. This was because my brother Morris gave Sammy his old clothes, and being a gambler, Morris was a very flashy dresser. So when Sammy wore Morris's clothes he looked like a seventeen-year-old gambler. And as long as he looked like one, he decided to be one. His first venture was on a Friday after he picked up his paycheck. He got into a crap game, and before he even got his hands on the dice he lost the whole fifteen dollars. After that Sammy didn't look like a gambler anymore; he had to sell Morris's clothes to get the thirteen dollars for my mother.

Eventually Sammy settled down and wound up running his own novelty store in one of the large hotels in Brooklyn. He's now retired and living with his wife, Sarah, and they have two fine children who are both teaching school. Sarah and Sammy have been married a long, long time, and even after all these years they have stuck to an arrangement they made before their wedding. Sarah was Italian, and she stayed Italian; Sammy was Jewish, and he stayed Jewish. I ate dinner at their house one night, and it was delicious, if you happen to like spaghetti on a bagel.

Recently their daughter, Dottie, treated Sammy and Sarah

to their first trip out of the United States: a tour of Israel and Rome. Living up to their original arrangement, they agreed to spend half their time in Israel and the other half in Rome. Frank Sinatra and Golda Meir couldn't have worked it out any better. After they returned I got this glowing letter from Sammy describing what a wonderful country Israel was. He was so impressed with how friendly the people were, how they had made the desert bloom with vegetation, the great advances they had made in education, the awesome feeling of standing in places where the history of the world began, etc., etc. Anyway, he went on for fifteen pages about Israel and never even mentioned Rome. I called him on the phone and said, "Sammy, that was a wonderful letter, but all you wrote about was Israel. What about Rome?"

Sammy answered, "If you want to know about Rome, I'll have Sarah write you a letter."

Within a week I got a seventeen-page letter from Sarah. She not only didn't mention Israel, she didn't mention Sammy.

Six months ago I was in New York, and Sammy and I were having lunch. I asked him, "Sammy, you're now about seventy-five or seventy-six years old. Looking back on your life is there anything you would have changed?"

"Just one thing," Sammy said. "If I knew I wouldn't get caught, I'd still like to be a detective."

My brother Willy was the youngest of the family. Now there was such a gap between the ages of Willy and my oldest brother, Morris, that for years Willy thought Morris was his grandfather. Willy also always thought of himself as quite a ladies' man. At the ripe old age of twelve he used to take soot from the stove and rub it on his face. He wanted the girls to think he was old enough to shave. And he was very skinny, so he wore his tie pulled up real tight around his neck, and that made his cheeks puff out. He looked like a squirrel with five-o'clock shadow.

Anyway, when he reached thirteen, one day he came home and announced to my mother that he was getting married. My mother went right along with it. "Good," she said, "who are you marrying?"

Willy said, "A girl named Gertie Moskowitz."

"This Gertie Moskowitz . . . how old is she?"

"She's eleven," Willy replied. "But don't worry, Mama, she's Jewish."

"That's nice," my mother said, "then you can get married next Sunday. We'll have the rabbi meet us at the soda fountain."

Needless to say, that marriage didn't take place, and needless to say, I sound pretty silly telling you that. However, at the age of twenty-three Willy did marry a very lovely girl named Louise, and they had three charming daughters.

Willy was the only one of my family who joined me in show business. He had a good business head, and when Gracie and I started doing well he became our personal manager. He handled all our contracts, our bookings, and traveled with us. Eventually, when we went into radio and then television, Willy even doubled as one of our writers. I don't know why, but there was one particular joke that Willy came up with that has stuck in my mind through the years. I've always enjoyed telling it and in fact, I still use it. And so you won't think I'm lying to you, I'll use it again right now. I was speaking at a testimonial dinner for Judy Garland, and this is what I said:

When Judy Garland was nine years old, the Trocadero restaurant on the Sunset Strip gave young talent a chance to perform every Sunday night. The night that Judy Garland sang there Louis B. Mayer, who was then the head of MGM, was sitting in the audience. He loved the way she sang, signed her to a contract and made her a star. Well, the same thing could have happened to me, but the only problem was when I was nine years old, Louis B. Mayer was nine years old.

Well, that was Willy's joke, and I'm telling it again next Wednesday. I only wish that Willy was still around to hear it. He passed away in 1966, and I still miss him very much.

Now I've told you a little bit about all my brothers and sisters. They were all married and all had children. And their children had children. And their children's children had children. By now I figure in some way or another I must be related to everybody in the United States. Believe me, if Alex Haley had my family, he'd still be writing *Roots*.

IT TAKES TWO PEOPLE TO MAKE A MARRIAGE

JANUARY 7, 1926, was the most important day in my life. That's when audiences discovered I had this big talent, and I stayed married to her for thirty-eight years. At that time getting married was so simple. At seven-thirty in the morning Gracie and I went to the Justice of the Peace; she said, "I do"; I said, "I do"; and we did.

But it's certainly not like that now. Just the other day I went to a wedding that wasn't even a wedding, it was a business meeting; just a few close friends, two lawyers, the boy and girl and their baby. They were there to sign a Marriage Contract. They didn't even say "I do," because there was nobody there to ask them. When kids get married today I don't know what they say. I guess it could be, "Perhaps" . . . "Maybe" . . . "I will, if you will" . . . "I'll try" . . . "Speak to my attorney!" . . . I hate to mention this because it might upset some of you readers, but I don't think that's very romantic.

Anyway, it was quite a ceremony. The two lawyers argued about some of the points in the contract and eventually arrived at a compromise. Then the lovers signed it and shook hands. How they got that baby I'll never know.

Imagine the boy and girl going home after having just been joined together by two lawyers. Now this is their wedding night. The music is playing softly, the lights are low, she's in a beautiful black negligee, he's in his silk pajamas, and they jump into bed, turn up the lights and start to read the contract. They're afraid that the next thing they do might not be legal.

Well, the contract probably reads something like this:

Whereas the Party of the First Part, for and in consideration of the covenants and agreements hereinafter mentioned, and to be performed by the Party of the Second Part, does hereby agree and consent to the Party of the Second Part privileges and considerations known and described as follows, to wit: . . .

By the time the kids tried to figure out what that meant I imagine the Party of the First Part was telling the Party of the Second Part that if there were any other parties with any other party, the whole party's over. (I don't know what I just said, but one thing I'm sure of is, the Party of the First Part and the Party of the Second Part didn't.) Of course, there must be a loophole somewhere in the contract that states if he catches her fooling around, the whole deal is off unless she's a good cook.

And I'm sure it wouldn't be a binding agreement without a clause pointing out that Tuesdays and Thursdays are for conjugal obligations, except on national holidays. Friday is his night out, but he always looks forward to Tuesdays and Thursdays, because those are his nights in.

Now being an old vaudevillian and having signed a few contracts in my day I'm certain the last paragraph says that the agreement is subject to renewal at the end of every two years; that is, if the parties are still speaking to each other.

By now no doubt you've come to the conclusion that I haven't got a law degree. I was in the fourth grade so long I wound up dating my teacher.

But getting back to that so-called wedding. After I witnessed the signing of the paper I took the two kids aside and asked them, "What kind of a wedding is this? Why don't you two really get married?"

Without blinking an eye, the boy said, "Oh, we love each other too much for that." And the girl chimed in with, "Sure, marriage has broken up more friendships than anything!"

Well, there I was stuck with two pockets full of rice. So I went home and made myself some rice pudding. And it was delicious. I've never had rice pudding with pocket lint before.

Now let's talk about that important day in my life, January 7, 1926. The week before that Gracie and I were booked to play a split week in Steubenville and Ashtabula, Ohio. They were small-time theaters, and the reason we booked them was to break in some new material. After that we were to play the B.F. Keith Theater in Cleveland, which was the big-time.

Before we left New York for Steubenville I said to Gracie, "We've got two days off in Cleveland before we open, how about getting married then?" I'll admit this wasn't a great romantic proposal, but I want you to know that I had proposed to Gracie at least four times a week for the last year. So I had used up all my good proposal stuff.

In case you think Gracie immediately said "yes," you're wrong. What she said was, "George, I love you, and I love Benny Ryan. He wants to marry me, and you want to marry me. I'm sorry, but I've got a date with Benny tonight, and when I get home I'll make up my mind and phone you."

What's the use of kidding, it didn't look good for me. Benny Ryan was tough competition. He was a tremendous talent, one of our top songwriters, a great dancer, an exciting performer— he was all of show business wrapped up in one man. And besides that, he and Gracie had a lot in common. They were both Irish, they were both Catholic, and they both had their own hair. When I said that things didn't look good for me, believe me I was bragging.

Waiting for Gracie's phone call, I didn't get any sleep that night. I kept looking at the gold wedding ring that I had been carrying around for a year in case Gracie ever said "yes." I figured there was twenty dollars going down the drain.

Well, at two-thirty in the morning the phone finally rang. I rushed to the phone and picked it up. It was a wrong number. That's all I needed. I went back and had my ninth cup of coffee to calm my nerves. At four o'clock the phone rang, and this time it was Gracie. She said, "George, I've been sitting home for a couple of hours thinking about this, and I've made up my mind. I love you, and I think Cleveland would be a wonderful place for you and me to get married."

I said, "Thanks, kid, you just saved me twenty dollars."

We got our wedding license between shows in Steubenville. I had made a reservation for a two-room suite at the Statler Hotel in Cleveland. It cost seven dollars a day, but I figured it was going to be our honeymoon, why not go all out. But unfortunately we arrived at the Statler at five o'clock in the morning. Check-in time was seven o'clock, so Gracie and I sat in the lobby for two hours so we wouldn't have to pay for an extra day. We couldn't even go into the coffee shop; it wasn't open yet. So there we were, sitting in this big empty lobby holding hands among the potted palms.

At seven o'clock I went up to the desk and registered as Mr. and Mrs. George Burns. I told the clerk to send our bags up to our rooms, that we were on our way to get married and would be right back. He smiled and gave me an understanding wink.

Well, Gracie and I hopped into a cab for the justice of the peace. On the way I said to her, "Did you notice that the clerk winked at me?"

She smiled and patted my hand and said, "Why not, George, you're a very attractive man."

Just as we pulled up to the office of the justice of the peace, he and a friend came out the front door. They both carried

Right, George's mother, Dora, taken around 1902.

Below left, his sister, Sarah, about 1909.

Below right, his sister, Theresa (right), with two friends in 1913.

Right, his mother, Dora (right), with his sister, Mamie.

Below left, his oldest brother, Morris, the ladies' man of the family.

Below right, his sister, Sarah, with her husband, Sam Weiss, and their children, Louis and Evelyn.

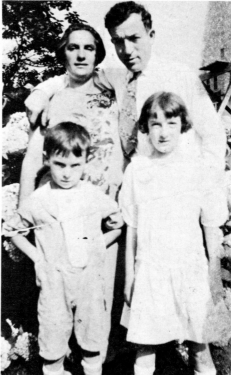

His darling mother, Dora, in a formal portrait, *above*, and in a snapshot taken around 1910, *right*.

Right, his sister, Goldie, with her daughter, Sally, holding Goldie's granddaughter, Karen, in the late 1940s.

His sister, Mamie, *below left*, when she was a kid of 70, and *right*, with George.

Above left, with his brother, Willie, and sister, Goldie, in the late 1950s.

Above right, his sister, Esther, taken early in 1959.

Below, his oldest brother, Isadore.

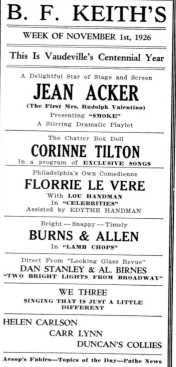

Left, George becomes a leading man for a day. PHOTOGRAPH AND PRESS BUREAU, INC.

Right, a vaudeville bill from Keith's Theatre, Philadelphia.

Burns and Allen in their early days of
vaudeville. WEISE STUDIO

Above, George breaks up as Gracie carries on a "perfectly normal" telephone conversation. *Facing page*, the proud parents with Ronnie and Sandra, 1936.

Above, with Ronnie and Sandra, 1940. METROPOLITAN PHOTO SERVICE

Right, Gracie and Sandra do a turnabout as George looks on, 1937. PARAMOUNT PICTURES, INC.

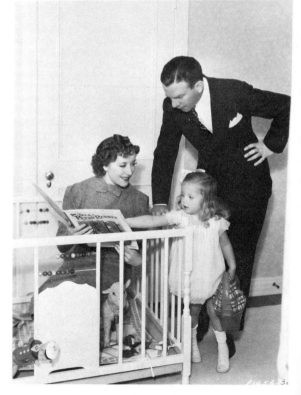

Left, Gracie and Ronnie are entertained by a budding puppeteer, Sandra, 1944. GENE LESTER

Below, with Ronnie and Sandra, 1950. HOLLYWOOD PICTORIAL SERVICE

Left, with Ronnie and Sandra at home posing for publicity pictures, 1952.

Below, with Ronnie, 1955.

With Ronnie and Sandra. *Right*, CBS PHOTO CREDIT BY WALT DAVIS

Above, Gracie and W. C. Fields in *International House* at Paramount in the early 1930s.

Below, a studio publicity photo in 1934. PARAMOUNT PRODUCTIONS, INC.

Above, with Guy Lombardo on the set of *Many Happy Returns*, 1934.
PARAMOUNT PRODUCTIONS, INC.

Below, with Cary Grant. GENE LESTER

Above, George takes a shower—
but no hot water, 1938. PARA-
MOUNT PICTURES, INC.

Right, George waiting impatiently
for Gracie to get a laugh.

fishing gear and were obviously on their way to go fishing. I rushed up to them and said, "We'd like to get married!"

He gave me a look, and said, "Why don't you come back tomorrow?" As they started off I stopped them again. "Please, Mr. Justice of the Peace," I said, "we traveled all night, we've got our license, we've checked into a hotel, and we've got to get married right away. The fish can wait, but we can't!"

I could see that I had won, because he stopped putting worms on his hook. With a resigned sigh he said to his friend, "Come on, Joe, it'll only take a few minutes. You'll have to stand up for this couple."

With that we all went inside the office, with Gracie nervously clutching my arm. The justice called to his wife to be a witness. She came out from the living quarters in the rear wearing bedroom slippers, a wraparound kimono, and her hair up in pin curls. Believe me, this wedding picture would never have made the society page. The only romantic thing about it was the faded flowers on the woman's kimono.

I don't remember much of anything about the ceremony. All I know is the justice of the peace stood there with a book in one hand and his fishing pole in the other. He said something to Gracie, then he said something to me. Gracie said, "I do," I said, "I do," and the Justice said, "I now pronounce you man and wife." I gave him ten dollars, and he was out of the front door before we were. To give you an idea of how long this took, when we arrived there the meter on the cab read eighty-five cents; when we got back into the cab it read ninety-five cents.

On our way back to the hotel Gracie snuggled up to me and gave me a big kiss. "Honey, we really did it," she said.

"Yeah," I said, taking her hand, "you're finally Mrs. George Burns."

She looked at me with a funny little gleam in her eye and said, "I hope so. For a moment I thought we were getting a fishing license."

When we got back to the hotel and went up to the desk, Gracie deliberately held out her finger with the wedding ring on it, and in a voice just loud enough for the clerk to hear, said, "George, you have exquisite taste, the wedding ring is just beautiful."

I said, "Thanks, Gracie, I'm glad you like it, I made it myself."

With that Gracie laughed and turned to the clerk. Sweetly she said, "Mr. and Mrs. George Burns would like the key to their rooms."

Well, we went upstairs and unpacked, and then we did what every young newly married couple does—we went downstairs and had breakfast. A little later my older brother and his family came over from Akron, and that evening we had a lovely wedding party in the hotel's main dining room. After they left Gracie and I went back to our rooms and started out as Mr. and Mrs. George Burns. We turned out the lights. . . . At two o'clock in the morning the phone rang. It was my dearest friend, Jack Benny, calling from Omaha. I recognized his voice instantly. I picked up the phone, and Jack said, "Hello, George—" and I said, "Send up two orders of ham and eggs" and hung up. Ten minutes later the phone rang and it was Jack again. I picked up the phone, and he said, "Hello, George—" and I said, "You forgot the ketchup" and hung up.

Maybe you think that was the end of it, but it wasn't. A half hour later there was a knock on the door and it was the waiter with two orders of ham and eggs and a bottle of ketchup. Trying to keep a straight face, the waiter said, "Compliments of Mr. Jack Benny from Omaha."

I said, "That's very nice of him, and I don't want to hurt Mr. Benny's image, so don't tell anybody I'm giving you a tip."

Gracie got up and we had our breakfast at two-thirty in the morning. The ham and eggs were delicious, and when we were finished Gracie said, "George, this was the high point of the night!" I hope she was making a joke.

Now as I said at the beginning of this chapter, January 7, 1926, was the most important day in my life. And even though it was a short wedding, and a short honeymoon, it was a long and wonderful marriage.

THEY PAID US IN POUNDS AND WEIGHED US IN STONES

FOR GRACIE AND me it was much tougher getting married than staying married. The hardest thing was trying to ignore the advice from some of our well-meaning friends. Come to think of it, it wasn't difficult at all, I just didn't listen. To give you an example, one week after we were married, Jack Holloway, another vaudeville actor, sat me down and very seriously told me I had made a big mistake. He said, "George, you know I love you, and I love Gracie. I don't know whether I should say this, but I feel I must say it because I'm one of your closest friends. . . . Your marriage can't last."

"But, Jack," I protested, "we just got married."

He said, "So far you've been lucky. Let's be honest, you and Gracie both come from different backgrounds. She's very well educated, and you had no schooling at all. Gracie comes from an Irish Catholic family in San Francisco, and you're from an Orthodox Jewish family on the Lower East Side of New York."

"Jack," I said, "I imagine you're telling me this because you love me."

"Would I be saying it if I didn't?" he said. Then he put his arm around my shoulder and added, "George, don't forget, you'll have to eat fish every Friday night."

I put my arm around his shoulder and told him not to worry. I said, "Jack, coming from an Orthodox family, on Friday night when I eat fish I'll keep my hat on."

He gave me a look and said, "George, I hope you're not trying to be funny. Because now I have to tell you something that I didn't want to tell you.

"That's because you love me."

"Of course," he said. "The reason your marriage won't last is that you and Gracie work together, and your careers are bound to clash. That's why I've never allowed my wife to go into show business."

I'd had enough. Very calmly I said to him, "Jack, I know how hard it was for you to tell me all this, and to show my appreciation . . . you can kiss my ass."

Just as a footnote, Gracie and I were happily married for thirty-eight years. Jack Holloway and his wife were divorced a year and a half later. In fact, the last time I saw him he was having a problem with his fifth wife. I guess this kid never learned to eat fish with his hat on.

But Gracie and I had no problems with our careers, because we only had one—hers. We stood in the wings, the orchestra played "Love Nest," we made our entrance holding hands, and when we got to center stage I said to Gracie, "How's your brother?" and she spoke for thirty-eight years. And that's how I became a star. Believe me, it wasn't easy; sometimes I forgot to say, "Gracie, how's your brother?"

Here I am tearing myself down again, but I do that on purpose. I found out that if you tear yourself down, people feel sorry for you, and if they feel sorry for you, they like you. But don't feel too sorry for me. When I was on the stage I did more than just say, "Gracie, how's your brother?" I also used to find out which way the wind was blowing, and I'd make sure to stand on the opposite side of Gracie so my cigar smoke wouldn't blow in her face. That was my real talent. You feel sorry for me again? . . . you see, it works.

Well, you're not going to believe this, but it's true. Gracie and I were playing the Palace Theater in New York, and at that time the hit musical was *Show Boat*. It was produced by Charles Dillingham and he was putting together the cast for his London production. He came to the Palace because he was considering us for the Eva Puck and Sammy White parts. Puck and White were the comedy leads in *Show Boat*, and this would have been a tremendous break for us. But when I found out Dillingham was in the audience I got so nervous I forgot to check out which way the wind was blowing. So when we did our act my cigar smoke went into Gracie's face. The next day our agent, Tom Fitzpatrick, got a wire from Charles Dillingham. It read, "The team of Burns and Allen I'll pay $500 a week. For the girl alone I'll pay $750." As you've probably guessed, the London *Show Boat* sailed without us.

As long as I've mentioned Tom Fitzpatrick, I'd like to tell you a little anecdote involving him. Tom Fitzpatrick was one of the top vaudeville agents. He handled a lot of good standard vaudeville acts, such as Jack Benny, Barry and Whitledge, Block and Sully, Will Mahoney, Swift and Kelley, Burns and Allen, and many others. Tom was very religious, and one of the kindest, warmest, most considerate men I ever met. In those days it was the practice of the various acts to go into their agent's office to find out if they were booked somewhere. But Tom was so soft-hearted he couldn't tell an actor that he had nothing for him. It was just impossible for him to say, "You're not working next week." So when you came into his office and there was no job, Tom got very nervous and started opening and closing drawers of his desk like he was looking for something. He just couldn't bring himself to face you. The minute he started that bit you knew you were laying off. And because he was such a nice man and you didn't want to hurt his feelings, you'd back out of his office and quietly close the door.

Well, one day after backing clear down into the street, I ran into Jack Benny. Jack said, "George, are you and Gracie working next week?"

I answered, "No, I just left Tom Fitzpatrick and he was opening and closing drawers."

I don't know why, but that struck Jack funny, and he started to laugh. Now I don't mind making Jack Benny laugh when I'm booked, but not when I'm laying off. So I said, "Jack, what are you laughing at? You know that Tom Fitzpatrick's been doing that drawer bit for years."

That made him laugh even more. And the more he laughed, the angrier I got. Finally I stopped three strangers, pointed to Jack, and very innocently said, "Why is this man laughing?"

They looked bewildered and said, "Don't you know him?"

I said, "No." Then I turned to Jack and said, "Mister, why are you laughing?" Well, this really broke Jack up. He started to walk away, holding his sides, and every time he looked back I gathered more people. I must have had about forty or fifty, and the bigger the crowd the more he laughed. Finally he couldn't stand it any longer, fell down on the sidewalk, and crawled into a shoe store.

The next day Jack said to me, "George, that lousy joke of yours cost me twelve dollars yesterday."

"Jack," I said, "relax, the shoes look fine."

Here I am jumping around, talking about Jack Holloway, Tom Fitzpatrick, Jack Benny . . . my sense of continuity is pathetic. But come to think of it, Shakespeare had a problem with his continuity, too. Willy jumped from *The Merchant of Venice* to *Henry VIII*, to *Richard III*, to *Julius Caesar*. He didn't care about continuity, so why should I?

So let's take another little jump. The week after Gracie and I were married we played the Jefferson Theater on fourteenth

Street in New York City. We were doing a new act called Burns and Allen in *Lamb Chops,* and all the bookers came to see us. We were a very big hit, and we were signed for five years with the Keith-Orpheum circuit. What a wedding present! And to make it even more exciting, the contract called for us to play the Palace Theater in New York. Right away I had my spats cleaned, and to top it off I bought something I'd never owned before . . . a cane with an engraved silver handle. I wanted to look like I was a classy performer. Gracie didn't have to buy anything; she always looked like a classy performer.

When you signed one of these contracts you worked a minimum of forty weeks a year. That meant you had twelve weeks open. But who wanted to lay off that long? Not me, I layed off until I was twenty-seven years old. So at the end of our first season when we were offered to play four weeks in London, I ran home and told Gracie. "Gracie," I said, "they want us to play four weeks in London!"

Gracie's eyes lit up, and she immediately started packing.

"Wait a minute," I said, "we're only offered four hundred dollars a week. That means we'll only make sixteen hundred dollars, and our passage on the *Leviathan* to London is twelve hundred dollars, because we're going first class."

She just kept right on packing.

"So you see, Gracie, after we pay our hotel bill and all our other expenses, we'll play four weeks," and laying it out, I said, "and we will lose two hundred dollars!"

"George, I'm packed!" she said.

Well, we signed the contract, but I was wrong about losing two hundred dollars. Gracie bought two evening gowns, because you had to dress every night on the *Leviathan.* So we were going to lose four hundred dollars.

Gracie and I were very excited about going to London because neither one of us had ever been there. Now this being my first trip out of the country, the one thing I didn't want to look like was an American tourist. I didn't want to walk down a

London street and have people staring at me. I wanted to look like an Englishman looks. Now it happened that I had recently seen an English vaudeville act called The Ward Brothers, and they billed themselves as, "Two British Chaps from London." I said to myself, that's it. I'll dress the way they dress, and when I get to London I won't be noticed.

My outfit consisted of a pair of gray-striped pants, a double-breasted black coat, an ascot instead of a regular tie, and a black bowler hat. Naturally I wore my spats, and instead of my cane I carried an umbrella. When I tried it all on at the tailor's I looked so English the clerk was surprised I didn't pay him in pounds.

The *Leviathan* was the largest and most magnificent luxury liner in the world at that time. Gracie and I couldn't believe that we would spend five days traveling to London in such style. As the ship pulled away we stood at the rail waving to our friends who were seeing us off. Lined up on the dock were about a dozen and a half of our friends, including Jack Benny, Mary Kelly, Orry Kelly, Jesse Block, Eva Sully, and our agent Tom Fitzpatrick. They were all smiling happily and waving. Gracie turned to me and made a little joke. She said, "They all look so happy, they must be glad to see us leaving." And being a good husband, I laughed.

We stayed at the rail until we passed the Statue of Liberty, and then we did what everybody did. We found out where we were sitting in the dining room, rented a couple of deck chairs, and strolled around the ship checking everything out. After that we went to our cabin and unpacked. We couldn't wait to get into our evening clothes for our first dinner aboard the *Leviathan*. But we made a mistake. What we didn't know was that on the first and last night aboard a big liner you don't dress for dinner. Those are the nights you unpack and pack.

Anyway, we weren't able to get dressed fast enough, and just as we were about to leave our cabin, Gracie said to me, "George, in that tuxedo you look perfect."

And I said, "Gracie, I've never seen you look lovelier than you do in that dress."

She smiled and said, "Thanks, George, I was waiting for you to say that; that's why I mentioned your tuxedo." And being a good husband, I laughed again.

Well, we nonchalantly walked into the dining room, just as if we had made this trip a thousand times before. Suddenly we froze in our tracks. It seemed that all conversation had stopped, and hundreds of eyes were upon us. Everyone else in the room was dressed in casual clothes.

Somehow Gracie and I got to our table and sheepishly sat down. Fortunately, we had a table for four, and the other couple were charming, wonderful, and understanding people. They introduced themselves as Dr. and Mrs. Graham Hamilton from Philadelphia, and they gave no indication whatsoever that there was anything peculiar about us. After we ordered cocktails, Dr. Hamilton said, "Would you excuse us for a moment. We forgot to send a cable, we'll be right back." And they left. As soon as they were out of sight, Gracie and I looked at each other and made a beeline for our cabin, where we changed into casual clothes. When we got back to the dining room there were the Hamiltons sitting at our table in their evening clothes.

Isn't that a nice story? Too bad it's not true. But you know me, I'm a vaudeville actor and I always think I need a finish. What really happened was, when Gracie and I came into the dining room 250 people thought they had made a mistake and rushed to their cabins and changed into their evening clothes. Now that's true. But if I had told you that at the beginning, you never would have believed it.

Well, the trip over was marvelous. The food was excellent, the shipboard activities were fun, Gracie and I never missed a dance, and for us it was a smooth and romantic crossing. However, on the second day out I was in the bar, having a drink and minding my own business, when somebody tapped me on the shoulder. I turned around and staring down at me was a tall, well-dressed man. He said, "You're George Burns, aren't you?" I nodded, and he continued, "I'm Big Charlie. Remember Hunt's Point Palace about fifteen years ago? . . . You and a girl gave an exhibition dance."

As I looked at him the whole thing came back to me. . . . Let me tell you what happened then. I was about sixteen years old, and I used to dance with a little girl named Nettie Gold. Every Friday night we gave an exhibition dance at different dance halls. Sometimes we would dance the Peabody, or the Machiche, but our big number was an "eccentric fox trot" that we did to a popular instrumental number called "Raggin' the Scale!" Well, this one night we were going to dance at Hunt's Point Palace, and Big Charlie came over to me and said, "Kid, what do they pay you for this dance?"

I said, "Five dollars."

"How long does the dance last?" Big Charlie asked.

"Oh, about three minutes."

"If you can make it last six minutes, I'll give you an extra ten dollars," Big Charlie offered.

I said, "Of course," and he handed me a ten-dollar bill. I thought to myself, this guy must really love the fox trot.

Just then our number was announced. Nettie danced in from one side of the hall, I danced in from the other, and when we got to the center of the floor a spotlight hit us as they turned the house lights out. I made the dance last a full six minutes. Nettie was a little confused, but she followed right along. Nettie was good. But what I didn't know was, while Nettie and I were doing six minutes so was Big Charlie. When the lights were out he picked everybody's pocket.

Now I've got a little confession for you. I did not split the ten dollars with Nettie. I didn't want her to feel guilty for accepting tainted money. . . .

Meanwhile, back on the *Leviathan*, Big Charlie and I were still staring at each other. I said, "Well, Charlie, it was nice to see you again," and started off.

He stopped me with, "By the way, George, are you still dancing?"

I said, "Yeah, but I don't do the eccentric fox trot anymore."

Later that night I told Gracie the story, and for the rest of our voyage part of our fun was avoiding Big Charlie.

When we arrived in London I was surprised . . . nobody dressed like the Ward Brothers. But since I'd made one mistake getting into the wrong clothes on the *Leviathan*, I certainly wasn't going to make another. So I never even unpacked my black coat and my gray-striped pants. But it wasn't a complete loss, because years later I gave the whole outfit to Georgie Jessel. And when he wore it he was a smash at funerals doing eulogies.

We were in London four days before we opened at the Victoria Palace. That was the big variety theater at that time. Gracie was the typical tourist. She had to see everything. She saw the changing of the guard at Buckingham Palace, Westminster Abbey, the Tower of London, Madame Tussaud's wax museum, whatever London had Gracie saw it . . . twice.

But not me. I was the typical vaudevillian. I ran right down to the theater to find out about the lights, about how many musicians they had, what dressing room we would be using, what side of the stage we'd make our entrance and what side we'd make our exit, and of course, which way the wind was blowing. Anyway, after checking everything out at the theater I went to Henry Sherek's office. He was my London agent, and I was going to meet him for the first time. He turned out to be a tall, very big man weighing about three hundred pounds. Our conversation started out with me saying, "I'm George Burns," and with him saying, "I'm Henry Sherek." I followed that with "You look great, you look like you've lost some weight." Then there was a long pause, and he said, "I hope your stuff on the stage is funnier," and I said, "It is." We both laughed, and we knew that the relationship was going to be a good one.

Well, Henry invited me that Saturday to play golf with Val Parnell, who booked all the top theaters in London and in the provinces. I was very anxious to meet Val Parnell, because although Gracie and I were in London for five weeks, we were only booked for four. We had a week open in between. I figured if I could fill that week, that would give us an extra four hundred dollars and we would break even; that is, if Gracie didn't go shopping again.

Val Parnell turned out to be a very nice man, but a very bad golfer. For the first four or five holes he was slicing, hooking, he was in sand traps, he was in the rough, he was all over the golf course except on the fairway. I could see that this put him in a bad mood, and it was no time for me to try to fill that extra week.

At that time I was not a good golfer, and now I'm even worse. But I had taken so many lessons that I knew how to help other people, even if I couldn't help myself. So I had a thought. On the sixth tee I said, "Mr. Parnell, I can't understand why you're not playing better golf. The most important thing about playing golf is to keep your head down and your eye on the ball. And you're certainly doing that." He wasn't, but this time when he hit his drive, he did.

As we were walking down the fairway I said, "That was a pretty good shot, Mr. Parnell. And no wonder, you always keep that left arm of yours nice and stiff." He didn't. But on the next shot he kept his head down, his left arm nice and stiff, and he hit a beautiful shot right to the green. And then he two-putted the green and got a par.

On the seventh tee he was all smiles and couldn't wait to hit his next shot. But before he did, I said to him, "Mr. Parnell, Gracie and I are booked here in London for four weeks, and we've got a week open on the fifteenth. That week we'd love to play the Shepherd's Bush Empire."

He said, "George, I'll tell you what. If I hit a ball 200 yards or better and stay on the fairway, the week at Shepherd's Bush Empire is yours." Well, he teed off, and God hit the shot for him. He split the fairway in half for about 215 yards. He turned to me in amazement, and said, "George the week of the fifteenth you and Gracie are playing the Shepherd's Bush Empire!"

"Thanks," I said, "and now, Mr. Parnell, I'd like to tell you something. You're the lousiest golfer I ever played with."

Henry Sherek quickly turned to Parnell and said, "Val, his stuff on the stage is funnier!" Parnell laughed, Henry Sherek laughed, and I was hysterical.

Well, that Monday we opened at the Victoria Palace. It's difficult for me to tell you exactly how we felt as we waited in the wings. This was the first time we had ever played to an audience outside the United States. Finally our music started, the spotlight hit the stage, and ready to make our entrance I took Gracie by the hand. I could tell immediately that she was nervous. All talented people get nervous. My hand was very steady. We walked out and did our fourteen minutes, and the English people loved Gracie as much as the Americans. We were a big hit. In fact, after taking three bows, we had to do an encore.

Now I'm not going to tell you what we did for fourteen minutes, but this was our encore: It consisted of sort of a stage argument. I would talk to the audience, and then Gracie would start talking to the audience. Then we'd both be talking to the audience at the same time. And we kept on talking until finally Gracie out-talked me. Sound confusing? I'll show you how it went:

GEORGE

Ladies and gentlemen, thank you very much,
and it's very exciting for us to play here in

London. We'd love to do a little more, but
we're not prepared.

GRACIE

I am.

GEORGE
(Continuing to audience)

It's really a thrill for us to be so well accepted
by you people.

GRACIE

I am.

GEORGE	GRACIE
I must tell you what happened when we found out we had been booked to play the Victoria Palace. Our Agent, Tom Fitzpatrick, told us that we were booked to play London for four weeks. We were thrilled, because although we had played in vaudeville all over America, we never dreamed that one day we'd be—	I am. If my brother Willie was here, I could do something alone if my brother was here. But my brother isn't here so I'll have to do something by myself. *(Turning to George)* My poor brother Willie, he was held up last night. Willie . . . my brother . . . was held up . . . last night . . . Willie . . . held up . . . my brother.

GEORGE
(Turning to Gracie)

Your brother.

GRACIE

He was held up.

GEORGE

Your brother was held up?

GRACIE

Yeah, by two men.

GEORGE

Where?

GRACIE

All the way home.

GEORGE

Your brother must drink a lot.

GRACIE

So does my brother.

GEORGE

Hasn't your mother ever tried to do something about your brother Willie's drinking?

GRACIE

She sent him to a psychiatrist, and the psychiatrist worked and worked to get to the bottom of his drinking, and finally he found out Willie's problem.

GEORGE

What was it?

GRACIE

He likes to drink.

GEORGE

So does my brother.

GRACIE

Hasn't your mother ever sent him to a—

GEORGE

Say good night, Gracie.

GRACIE

Good night.

Well, that was our encore, but opening night it didn't go quite that way. In the middle of it while Gracie and I were talking at the same time, a man in the seventh row, he must have been about six feet four, slowly stood up. He kept snapping his fingers and calling out, "Young man! Young man!"

We stopped right in the middle of the routine. I couldn't figure out what was happening, and I said to him, "Yes, sir?" And pointing to me, in a firm voice he said, "I think it would be very nice if you would let that charming little lady carry on," and he sat down.

I was so stunned I didn't know what to say. Stammering, I said, "All right, I'll let this . . . this charming little lady carry on, but . . . but it won't do any good because I don't know where I am now."

Without missing a beat, Gracie said, "I do."

I said "What?!"

She continued, "I do."

I said, "You do?"

"Yeah," she said, "my brother. My poor brother Willie, he was held up last night by two men. . . ."

Yes, we finished the routine, and the audience loved it. In

fact, we were such a big hit I even made the man in the seventh row take a bow.

We played our five weeks, and London loved us! And we loved London! And I loved Gracie! And Gracie loved me! And we both loved show business! Now with all that love I think it's time to end this chapter.

SHE WAS REALLY SOMETHING

WHEN WE RETURNED from London we opened our season at the Majestic Theater in Chicago. And we were such a big hit at the opening matinee that the manager moved us from the No. 4 spot to the No. 7 spot on an eight-act vaudeville bill. A comedy act can't be paid a greater compliment than that. Everything seemed to be going right. Ahead of us was forty weeks of big-time vaudeville and then, out of the clear sky I got a wire saying that my mother had died. I told the manager to get another act to replace us, and that night Gracie and I got on a train for New York. It shouldn't have come as such a shock to me because my mother was sixty-nine years old and had been bedridden for three years. But no matter how you prepare yourself for the inevitable the shock is still there.

We had eight hours on the train before we reached New York and I thought I should prepare Gracie for what would be going on when we arrived at my mother's house. I told her, "Gracie, my mother was the backbone that held my family together all these years. And with seven sisters and five brothers, you're going to hear a lot of crying. And when you add all of their families, the weeping and wailing will be like something you never heard before in your life. So when it happens be ready for it, that's the way we Jewish people express our grief."

She looked at me and patted my hand. "Don't worry, George," she said, "we Catholics shed a few loud tears ourselves."

I didn't get much sleep on the train that night. I kept thinking of how my mother's wisdom and strength had shaped my family. She had many wonderful qualities, but most of all I loved her sense of humor. It was never direct, it was always by inference. I remember one incident in particular. It was the first time Gracie and I played the Palace Theater in New York. My mother had then been bedridden for about two years. We had two more days left to finish the week, and early Saturday morning I went to visit her. The first thing she asked was, "How are you and Gracie doing at the Palace?"

"Just great, Mama," I answered.

She sort of sighed and said, "You know, Nattie, I've been waiting for years to see you play the Palace, and now you're there, and here I am."

Trying to cheer her up, I jokingly said, "Mama, I'll tell you what we'll do. Tomorrow I'll hire a limousine, and the girls can help you get ready. Then Sammy and Willy will help you to the car and go to the theater with you. We'll time it so you get there right after intermission. You'll see Gracie and me, and Elsie Janis who's the headliner, and then Sammy and Willy will get you back into the car and we'll all drive back to Brooklyn. How would you like that?"

"I'll wear my blue dress," she said.

I was knocked over: I didn't think she'd take me seriously. But I was delighted. I was also worried if she was strong enough to make it. But she made it. The next day at the Palace she saw Gracie and me, and Elsie Janis. And I must say, Gracie and I were never better. After the show Sammy, Willy, and I drove Mama back to Brooklyn. On our way, I proudly turned to her and said, "Mama, who was the best on that bill?"

She said, "First came Elsie Janis. Then came Gracie."

That wasn't exactly what I expected to hear. "But, Mama," I said, "what about me?"

She smiled and said, "Nattie, I said it before, and I'll say it again. You're a nice boy."

Lying there in my berth, with the train rolling towards New York, it made me feel good that my mother finally saw me at the Palace. But it saddened me to realize I would never again hear her say, "Nattie, you're a nice boy."

Well, the next morning Gracie and I arrived at my mother's house on Carroll Street in Brooklyn. As we were walking in Gracie took my hand. When I opened the door the house was full of all my brothers and sisters, and some relatives I'd never even seen before. But I got the surprise of my life. I looked at Gracie; I couldn't believe it. Nobody was crying. There was sadness and quiet conversation, but none of that weeping and wailing I had expected. After Gracie and I said hello to my family I took my sister Mamie aside. "Mamie," I said, "I'd like to ask you something."

She said, "I know exactly what you're going to ask me. Mama didn't want anyone to cry."

After the funeral I found out why. You see, my brothers Sammy and Willy were the only ones still living at home, and the night before my mother passed away she called them into her room and told them she was going to die. Naturally, they didn't believe her. But she insisted. "Boys," she said, "remember three years ago when I got very sick and everybody thought I was going to die. I didn't. I wasn't ready. Now I am."

There was a slight pause, then she continued. "Sammy, Willy, I want you both to sit down here on the bed and listen. All my life I prayed for one thing, that when it was time for me to leave this earth I wanted to be in my right mind. And my prayers have been answered." A little smile, then, "Now I want you to call your sisters and have them come over early in the morning. I want the house spic and span. And tell Goldie to make sure that the coffee is very hot. You know Uncle Frank, if the coffee isn't hot he won't go to the funeral." Another pause, "Now boys, this is very important. I don't want any crying. Be sure to tell everybody. I don't want any crying. And I know you'll all sit shiva* for a week. Nattie will be coming in from Chicago, and he's very busy and he's got to get back to work. I know he's not very religious, but tell him to sit shiva for a half hour, it won't hurt him. Now boys, do you understand?"

They both nodded yes, and Sammy said, "Here, Mama, take this medicine and rest a little. You'll feel better in the morning."

"All right, Sammy," Mama said, "I'll take the medicine."

In the morning when my brothers walked into her room it was just as she had said—Mama had left us.

Well, I sat shiva for four days. I wanted to sit shiva for a week, but I couldn't. Gracie and I had to open the following week in Milwaukee. On the train to Milwaukee I turned to Gracie and said, "My mother was really something, wasn't she?"

Gracie said, "Yes, she certainly was a great lady." Then she leaned over and gave me a little kiss. "And George, you're a nice boy."

*For those of you who may not know what "sitting shiva" means, in the Orthodox Jewish religion after the funeral the immediate family sits in the house of the deceased for seven days, giving up all comforts, as a token of respect.

TITLES CAN DRIVE YOU NUTS

I'VE SAID THIS before, but I'm going to say it again because I really believe it, and I think it's very important. And when something is important you can say it ten times, twenty times, fifty times, if you believe it. And I believe it, so I'll keep saying it and saying it. In fact, I've got to keep saying it because my publisher insists this book have at least three hundred pages.

What I'm trying to say is that if you're in love with what you're doing, failures can't stop you. When I was a kid I was always singing, but nobody liked it, so I started dancing, and nobody liked it. Then I started telling jokes, and nobody laughed. Then I tried to be dramatic, and everybody laughed. So I figured as long as I couldn't be a singer, or a dancer, or a comedian, or a dramatic actor, there was only one thing left for me to do. And I did it—I went into show business. By the time I found out I had no talent I was too big a star to do anything else.

I must admit that to make it, luck and timing are big factors, especially timing. I went from one failure to another until I was twenty-seven years old. And I hate to brag, but I wouldn't have had so many failures if my timing hadn't been perfect. But all those failures did teach me something. Eventually I must run out of them. And I did when I met Gracie. Now I'm not going to tell you how I met her, I've told that a thousand times. But if at the end of the book I'm short a few pages, I'll tell it again.

But now I want to tell you how luck played a big part in our career. It happened one night when Gracie and I were in the right place at the right time. It was at a party given by Arthur Lyons, one of our top theatrical agents in New York, who at that time represented Jack Benny. The only reason Gracie and I were invited was because we were friends of Jack. Well, during dinner Arthur came over to our table and told Jack that he had booked Fred Allen to make a short for Warner Brothers in Brooklyn the next day, but he just had a phone call telling him that Fred was sick and couldn't make it. He wound up saying, "Jack, I know you're busy, but can you suggest somebody? I need him right now."

While Jack was thinking I piped up with, "I can suggest somebody."

Arthur said, "Who?"

I said, "How about George Burns and Gracie Allen?"

Arthur thought about this for a moment. "Look," he said, "you have to be at Warner Brothers-Vitaphone in Brooklyn in your makeup at nine o'clock in the morning. You've got to do nine minutes, and you'll get seventeen hundred dollars. Do you think you can do it?"

"Arthur," I said, "for seventeen hundred dollars Gracie and I can not only do nine minutes, but we can drink a glass of water at the same time." As I said earlier, luck plays a big part. We were at the right place at the right time.

The next morning at eight o'clock we were at Warner Brothers putting on our makeup. There was a knock on our door and in came a man who looked very, very familiar. He told me he was Murray Roth. Well, I couldn't believe it. I hadn't seen Murray for years; we went to public school together, P.S. 22. After I introduced him to Gracie I asked him what he was doing there.

"The same thing you're doing," he said, "I'm in show business."

I said, "Murray, how could you be in show business? When we were in the fourth grade together you couldn't even sing harmony."

Murray laughed and said, "George, I'm a director. I'm directing you and Gracie in the short you're doing."

I said, "You're kidding. You, a director? You couldn't even find your way to the boys' room!"

"George," he said, "I've been directing shorts for two years now."

"Murray, I still don't believe it."

He said, "George, would I have my hat on backwards if I wasn't a director?"

That convinced me, and it also made me a little nervous. But then came the real problem. When we got on the stage I saw that the set they had built for Fred Allen was the interior of a living room. Well, that didn't fit Gracie and me at all, because the routine that we were going to do took place on a street corner. It took me a few minutes to solve the problem, and I'd like to show the way we did it.

Our director, Murray Roth, called, "Lights!" and the lights came up. Then he called, "Camera!" and the camera started clicking. Then he hollered, "Action!" and Gracie and I made our entrance into Fred Allen's living room. Gracie immediately started looking into the candy dish, the cigarette box, under the pillows, opening and closing drawers, etc.

GEORGE

Gracie, what are you looking for?

GRACIE

The audience.

GEORGE

You see that camera, you see the little lens
sticking out. Well, you look right into that
and that's where the audience is.

GRACIE

Oh? All right.

GEORGE

Now, Gracie, if we can talk for nine minutes,
they'll pay us seventeen hundred dollars. Do
you think you can do that?

GRACIE

George, just ask me what my brother Harvey
is doing.

Well, that started her, and she talked for nine minutes. In
the middle of a joke I stopped her:

GEORGE

Gracie, our nine minutes are up, and we just
made seventeen hundred dollars. Now wave
goodbye to the audience.

With that she waved, and I waved, and Murray Roth said,
"Cut!" Murray was right, he was a director.

Don't ask me why, but that short for Warner Brothers was a
big hit. It might have been because of our honest approach, or
maybe it was Fred Allen's living room, or Murray Roth saying
"Cut!" but before we knew it Paramount Pictures signed us for
four shorts at thirty-five hundred dollars a short. That meant
that Gracie and I made an extra fourteen thousand dollars a
year. In comparison our vaudeville salary looked very small,

even though we were getting five hundred dollars a week. But with this extra money coming in, and the short being such a big hit, I got very brave. I went to see Mr. Gottfried of the B.F. Keith office and told him that Gracie and I were very unhappy with our salary. Instead of five hundred dollars we now wanted seven hundred and fifty dollars a week. Gottfried stared right at me and said, "You and Gracie are not worth seven hundred and fifty dollars a week."

Full of our success, I stared right back and said, "Mr. Gottfried, you tell us why we're worth five hundred dollars a week and we'll forget the whole thing." He couldn't, so we got seven hundred and fifty dollars.

Well, Gracie and I were really moving up fast now. In fact, with all that money coming in I had my shoes shined whether they needed it or not. The first short was scheduled to be filmed at the end of our current road tour. So in between shows I started writing. I told Gracie I had a good idea for our first short where she played a salesgirl, but I just couldn't think of a title. For two days I sat there racking my brain, and then finally it came to me. I rushed into Gracie's dressing room and said, "Gracie, I've got the title!"

She stopped putting on her makeup and turned to me. "What is it?" she said.

"'The Salesgirl,'" I said proudly.

"George," Gracie said, "you're a nice boy," and she continued putting on her makeup.

Well, it wasn't easy for me to be a writer. I had to write everything in longhand. And as I said, I only went as far as the fourth grade in P.S. 22 and I was a very bad speller. And that was my best subject. So when I started being a screenwriter I had to spell everything phonetically. Then I would give what I had written to Gracie and she translated it back into English. Working out the idea and getting it down on paper, I was lucky if I finished a page a day. And to complete the short I needed at least twenty-five pages. So you see, Gracie had to do a lot of correctıng, and not once did she ever mention my spelling. Now that's true love.

We finished our tour and went to Astoria on Long Island, where Paramount had their studio, to do our first short. And who do you think was our director? Sid Garfield. No, Murray Roth wasn't there anymore. Somebody turned his hat around and he became one of the top producers.

Well, this is what I came up with. Here it is:

(The scene takes place at a cigar counter in a hotel lobby)

PARAMOUNT PICTURES

Presents

GEORGE BURNS AND GRACIE ALLEN

In

"THE SALESGIRL"

(A telephone rings, and Gracie, behind the cigar counter, picks up the phone)

GRACIE

Hello. Oh hello, Mary, I was just going to call you. When are you giving me the surprise party? . . . Tuesday night . . . Sure I've got a new dress, I'm wearing it . . . What time Tuesday night? . . . Oh, you can't tell me, that's the surprise. . . . Sounds like fun. Tuesday night, don't forget to be there. . . . Goodbye.

(She hangs up as a customer comes up to the counter)

CUSTOMER

I'll have two of those cigars.

GRACIE

That'll be twenty cents.

CUSTOMER

Here's five dollars.

(She gives him the cigars and rings up the money)

GRACIE

Anything else?

CUSTOMER

Yes, four-eighty.

GRACIE

We haven't got cigars for four-eighty.

CUSTOMER

Who wants cigars for four-eighty? I want two cigars for twenty cents.

GRACIE

I think you're silly to pay four-eighty for cigars that only cost twenty cents.

CUSTOMER

(Exasperated)

Four-eighty! Twenty cents! I don't want any cigars! Here's your cigars, now give me back my five dollars!

GRACIE

Oh, we never refund money, and besides you had no right to leave the counter before counting your change.

CUSTOMER

Leave the counter, count my change!! I didn't leave the counter, I didn't get any change!!

GRACIE

Look, am I going to have the same trouble with you I had yesterday. I'm going to call the house detective.

(Calls)

Mr. Sweeney! Mr. Sweeney!
(Mr. Sweeney, a big, tall, burly man, enters)

SWEENEY

Yes, Miss Allen, what is it?

(She gives him the two cigars)

GRACIE

Here, have two cigars.

SWEENEY

Oh, I couldn't, Miss Allen.

GRACIE

Take them, they're paid for.
(He takes them)

SWEENEY

Thanks. Now, what's the problem?

GRACIE

Mr. Sweeney, this man bought two cigars for twenty cents and gave me five dollars. How much do I owe him?

SWEENEY

Four dollars and eighty cents.

GRACIE

And four-eighty from five dollars is how much?

SWEENEY

Twenty cents.

GRACIE

And how much are two cigars at ten cents apiece?

SWEENEY

Twenty cents.

GRACIE

Then doesn't that make us even?

SWEENEY

Yes, I guess it does.

GRACIE

Then throw this crook out. . . .

SWEENEY

Come on, get out of here.

(He drags the customer off)

GRACIE

(Calling after them)

I should have known yesterday I was going to have trouble with you today!

(George enters)

GEORGE

Hello, Gracie.

GRACIE

Hello, George. Don't forget the party Tuesday night.

GEORGE

Gracie, it's supposed to be a surprise.

GRACIE

Oh, you spoiled it for me. . . .

GEORGE

I'm sorry. Let me have two cigars for twenty cents.

(He gives her twenty cents. She rings it up and gives him the cigars)

GRACIE

Here's your four-eighty change.

GEORGE

Gracie, you're a little mixed up. I didn't give you five dollars. I gave you twenty cents.

GRACIE

Now listen, am I going to have the same trouble with you I had with that other fellow.

GEORGE

Not with me. I can use four-eighty. I haven't got a cent, I'm a pauper.

GRACIE

You're a what?

GEORGE

I'm a pauper.

GRACIE

Oh, congratulations, boy or girl?

GEORGE

I really don't know.

GRACIE

Well, you better find out. Your brother will want to know if he's an uncle or an aunt.

GEORGE

I'll phone him when I get home. . . . Say, Gracie, do you know who you remind me of?

GRACIE

I know, I was taken once for Clara Bow.

GEORGE

Well, that's show business. . . . You were taken once for Clara Bow, and I was taken for grand larceny.

GRACIE

George, don't be silly, you don't look a bit like him. . . .

GEORGE

He's sort of a big, tall blond fellow.

GRACIE

I know, and he's a very good dancer.

GEORGE

Say, you've got a pretty nice job here.

GRACIE

Job? I could have had two jobs. This one at ten dollars a week and another one at forty dollars a week.

GEORGE

Then why did you take this job?

GRACIE

Because I figure that if I lose a ten-dollar job instead of a forty-dollar job, I'll be saving thirty dollars.

GEORGE

Look, at thirty dollars a week, at the end of the year you'll have saved yourself fifteen hundred dollars.

GRACIE

Sure, if I'm out of work for ten years, I'll have enough money to retire.

GEORGE

Do you mind if I change the subject?

GRACIE

No, this is a free country.

GEORGE

That's a nice dress you have on.

GRACIE

I'm glad you like it. It's my party dress for Tuesday night. My sisters, Jean and Alice, are going, too. They're twins, you know.

GEORGE

I didn't know you had twin sisters.

GRACIE

They really should be triplets, because I think Alice is two-faced.

GEORGE

Do they look exactly alike?

GRACIE

Oh yeah.

GEORGE

Is it hard to tell them apart?

GRACIE

Standing up or sitting down?

GEORGE

What difference does that make?

GRACIE

Well, we noticed when Alice sits down and Jean stands up—

GEORGE

Jean seems taller.

GRACIE

Yeah. . . . Even though they look exactly alike it's easy to tell them apart because Alice is married.

GEORGE

And Jean is single.

GRACIE

No, Jean is married, too.

GEORGE

Well, how do you tell them apart?

GRACIE

Jean is the one who has a swimming pool.

GEORGE

And Alice?

GRACIE

She sleeps on the floor.

GEORGE

She sleeps on the floor?

GRACIE

She's got high blood pressure and she's trying
to keep it down.

GEORGE

But Jean is the one with the swimming pool.

GRACIE

Yeah, we were there yesterday and we had
such fun. We were diving, and doing back
flips, and we'll even have more fun tomorrow
when they put water in it.

GEORGE

Well, exercise is good for you.

GRACIE

That's why we took the old woman with us.

GEORGE

Your mother?

GRACIE

No, the old woman who lives with us. She's been with us for five weeks now.

GEORGE

Is it your aunt?

GRACIE

We don't even know her. She just wanders around the house and does anything she wants.

GEORGE

Now let me get this. There's an old woman who wanders around your house and does anything she wants, and you don't even know her?

GRACIE

Sure. You see, my sister bought a ticket.

GEORGE

A ticket?

GRACIE

You see, they ran a raffle for a poor old woman, and—

GEORGE

Your sister won.

GRACIE

Yeah. . . .

GEORGE

Gracie, let's talk about anything except your
family.

GRACIE

Then you don't want to talk about my
brother.

GEORGE

No.

GRACIE

You're sure.

GEORGE

Yeah.

GRACIE

He's very tall, you know.

GEORGE

Gracie, I don't want to talk about your
brother.

GRACIE

He's an undercover agent.

GEORGE

An undercover agent? Is he in the secret
service?

GRACIE

No, he knows about it.

GEORGE

Maybe I shouldn't have asked.

GRACIE

Last week he went out on a murder case, and do you know he found that man in an hour.

GEORGE

He found the murderer in an hour?

GRACIE

No, the man who was killed.

GEORGE

Not only is your brother tall, but he's fast.

GRACIE

Oh yeah . . . And then Mr. & Mrs. Jones were having matrimonial trouble, and my brother was hired to watch Mrs. Jones.

GEORGE

Well, I imagine she was a very attractive woman.

GRACIE

She was, and my brother watched her day and night for six months.

GEORGE

Well, what happened?

GRACIE

She finally got a divorce.

GEORGE

Mrs. Jones?

GRACIE

No, my brother's wife.

GEORGE

Gracie, I've enjoyed every minute of it, but we've run out of time. So just wave goodbye to everybody.

GRACIE

Don't you want to hear about my Aunt Clara?

GEORGE

No.

GRACIE

She's not only tall, but she's fat.

GEORGE

I don't want to hear about her.

GRACIE

She's the one who collects all the clothes.

GEORGE

Gracie, we'll do that in our next short.

GRACIE

Do you promise?

GEORGE

I promise.

GRACIE

Good. Then I'll wave and say goodbye to everybody. Goodbye, everybody.

(As Gracie waves into camera, the picture fades out as music comes up)

THE END

(Written by George Burns, "Whiz Bang"
and "College Humor")

Well, we kept making shorts for Paramount. And during this time we also went into radio, and we did very well. Then in 1932 Paramount brought us to Hollywood for our first feature film, *The Big Broadcast*. And all this happened because we were in the right place at the right time. So all of you young kids who are trying to make it in show business, here's the way to do it. Wait until vaudeville comes back, work up an act with a very talented Irish girl who can spell, and make sure you're invited to an Arthur Lyons party.

SO WE STOPPED WORKING AND WENT INTO RADIO

In the last couple of years I've been interviewed a lot. Now some of these interviews turn out good, and some of them don't. A lot of it depends on the questions. If the questions are stale, the answers are stale, and if the questions are fresh, the answers are fresh. Sometimes when you hear some of my fresh answers you're better off with the stale questions.

A few years ago Henry Edwards of *The New York Times* asked me an interesting question. He wanted to know if during our careers did Gracie and I have a problem going from one medium to the other. I told him I hadn't thought of it before. When Gracie and I were in vaudeville we did a man and woman talking act, and when we went into radio, although you didn't see us, we were still talking. Then on television where you did see us, we were still talking. And in motion pictures where we were ten times the size, we were still talking. I wound up by saying, "So Henry, for Gracie and me it was very easy to go from one medium to the other; we just kept talking. And now I'll let you in on a little secret, but this is off the record. I found out there's quite a lot of money in talking."

Anyway, it turned out to be a good interview because Henry

asked the right questions. The problem was we were both enjoying it so much that we didn't notice the time. I happened to look at my watch just as Henry asked this question, "George, you've been in show business all your life. How important are entrances and exits?"

"Very important," I said, "especially an exit." Then taking another look at my watch, "Henry, it's a quarter after seven, and I've got a date with a twenty-two-year-old girl. Now if you don't leave right now, that girl is going to be too old for me." That got a laugh from Henry. He picked up his hat, and as I walked him to the door, I said, "Henry, you are now making what I would call a great exit."

But Henry had brought up one very important point: the difficulty of going from vaudeville into radio. Some acts couldn't make it, like jugglers, acrobats, tight-rope walkers, Duncan's Collies, Power's Elephants, Madame Burkhardt's Cockatoos, Swain's Cats & Rats, Fink's Mules, and of course, Dainty Marie.

Radio was really revolutionary. For the first time people did not have to come to the theater to see you. You entertained them by coming right into their living rooms. We reached millions of people in one night. So overnight we performers got to be sensations; we all got to be stars. What I realize now is that it wasn't us at all, the invention was the sensation. If it wasn't for that little crystal set, I'd still be playing Altoona.

For instance, when Gracie and I had been on radio for a couple of weeks, we were walking down Broadway and a man stopped us. "Aren't you Burns and Allen?" he asked. We said we were, and he continued, "I heard you last night all the way from Cleveland," and he walked away. Gracie and I exchanged looks, and just then the man came back and added, "I can also get Philadelphia on my set."

I said, "Thank you, that's quite a compliment."

Another time Gracie and I were having breakfast at Lindy's restaurant, and after the waiter took our order, he said, "I heard your show last night on my new Atwater Kent." I said, "How'd you like it?" and he replied, "Like it, it's a great set! If I were you, I'd get one." When he left I said to Gracie, "Remind me to give this kid a big tip."

One night Gracie and I went to see Victor Moore and Billy Gaxton in the Broadway show *Of Thee I Sing*. We loved it, and during the intermission we were standing in the lobby discussing it. Gracie was talking about how she was enjoying the show when there was a tap on her shoulder. She turned around, and this woman, bubbling with excitement, said, "You're Gracie Allen, right?"

"That's right," Gracie said.

Getting very friendly, the woman said, "I recognized your voice. Now you're not going to believe this story, it really is amazing. Last week I heard you on my radio set in Syracuse, and my sister in Denver heard you tell the same jokes on her set."

"Did you like that routine about Gracie's brother Harvey?" I ventured.

"Oh, I don't remember the jokes," she said, "but the most wonderful thing is that you both came through so clear."

When Gracie and I went back to see the second half of the show we still enjoyed Billy Gaxton and Victor Moore. And the reason we enjoyed them is they came through so clear.

In those days we never had a rating problem. We were all in the Top Ten—there were only eight shows. But eventually the newness of the machine wore off, the static cleared up, and people started to pay attention to the performers. A lot of new shows were developed, the quality of the writing improved, studio audiences were added to give it more excitement, broadcasting stations sprang up all over the country, and eventually radio became a fully developed form of entertainment. And before you knew it, the audience of millions and millions of people had created their radio stars.

With radio, success came so fast that it not only went to your head, it went to your neck, to your shoulders, to your chest, and I don't want to get risqué. People would now stop us on the street and ask for our autographs. When we went into restaurants we always got the best table. There were fan clubs, radio columnists, articles in magazines, newspaper interviews. In fact, there were publications devoted exclusively to radio personalities. Within a short time we were known all over the United States.

When I look back, I was so full of myself, of my own importance, and I was taking credit for things I had nothing to do with. The writers would write the script, and I'd give it to the producer. The producer would read it and say, "George, a very funny script," and I'd take a bow and say "Thank you." Then there was the sound effects man. He opened doors, he closed doors, he rang the telephone, he picked up the receiver, he put back the receiver, he made it rain, he made it thunder, he cried like a baby, he barked like a dog, he neighed like a horse, he meowed like a cat, he made things fall out of a closet—and I kept taking bows.

It was so easy for Gracie and me. What did we actually do? Our announcer, Bill Goodwin, would say, "Here they are . . . George Burns and Gracie Allen!" Then they'd hold up the "applause" sign, the audience would applaud, and Gracie and I would keep taking bows. We stood there with scripts in our hands, and I'd read the first line. "Gracie, say hello to everybody." Then Gracie would read her line, "Hello," and that's the way it went. If the writers would think of any ad libs, we'd write them down on the script. If you got so you could read your ad libs without rattling the paper, you were a great performer.

But one day I came up with an idea that worked. I took the sound effects man and made him a character on our show. He was played by a fine actor, Eliott Lewis, who later turned out to be one of our top directors. The idea of the character was that this sound effects man was a college graduate, and he found the job beneath him. For instance, in the script he would open the door, but before he slammed it shut he'd mutter, "Here I am a Phi Beta Kappa and this is what I do for a living!" And then, Bang! he'd slam the door. Another time he would make the telephone ring, but before he would pick up the receiver he'd mumble, "Four years of political science and my kids have to tune in to hear me do this!" and then he'd pick up the receiver.

The character really caught on for us. But one of my favorite bits on the show was when he said, "Mr. Burns, I've been working very hard, and I finally came up with a brand new sound effect. Maybe you can use it. It's a Siamese cat walking across a Persian rug."

I said, "Let me hear it."

After ten seconds of absolute silence, he asked, "How'd you like it?"

"I didn't hear anything," I said.

"Then it works," he said. "Thanks, it took me a long time to perfect it."

Now that got a very big laugh. But when I just read it over it doesn't sound funny. However, as I said, this book needs three hundred pages.

There were things that happened in radio that are amusing when I think of them now, but they could have turned into a disaster then; that is, if it weren't for one thing. Gracie and I had an understanding between us. The minute I said, "Gracie, let's talk about your brother," that meant forget the script and go right into our vaudeville routine. Let me give you a few examples of how it worked. Once we were doing a radio show in downtown Los Angeles, and about two minutes into the show for some reason the lights went out. Well, I immediately said, "Gracie, let's talk about your brother," and without missing a beat she answered, "Which brother do you want to talk about, the one who's in love or the one who sleeps on the floor?" We continued the routine until the lights came back on and then we started reading our scripts again.

Sometime later we were broadcasting from the CBS studios on Sunset Boulevard, and at that time Gracie and I used one microphone and read from the same script. Well, just as the show started someone in the control booth waved to Gracie. Gracie, who had the script in her hand, waved back and forty pages flew all over the place. Gracie turned to me and said, "Which brother do you want to talk about, the one who's in love or the one who sleeps on the floor?"

These two incidents were mild compared to what happened on the *Rudy Vallee Show* back in New York. Gracie and I were just beginning in radio and an appearance on the *Rudy Vallee Show*, which was one of the top shows, was a big break for us. Now just before the broadcast began my optometrist delivered my new pair of reading glasses. You guessed it; he gave me somebody else's glasses. I put them in my pocket and waited for our entrance. Well, we got this beautiful introduction from Rudy Vallee and walked out to the microphone with our scripts. I put on my glasses and of course I couldn't see a thing. I turned to Gracie and said, "Gracie, let's talk about your brother."

This time Gracie was stunned; she didn't know what had gone wrong. "Are you sure?" she whispered.

I took off my glasses and showed them to her. "I can't see a thing," I whispered back.

"Of course you can't," she murmured, "you've got your glasses off."

"Gracie," I whispered meaningfully, "the optometrist gave me the wrong glasses!"

With that Gracie said, "Which brother do you want to talk about, the one who's in love or the one who sleeps on the floor?" We did our six minutes and were a riot. But poor Rudy Vallee spent the entire time looking through the script trying to find out where we were.

Now let me backtrack a little and tell you how Gracie and I got started in radio. Oddly enough it wasn't in America, it was in London. We were playing the variety theaters and we got an

offer from the British Broadcasting Company to do five broadcasts. We didn't take radio too seriously then, so we weren't too
impressed. But what did impress us was that we would make an
extra hundred pounds so naturally we accepted. They wanted
us to do a routine lasting about six minutes. And the way it
worked we did the same routine for all five broadcasts. Since at
that time there was no network, our first broadcast, on a
Monday, was heard only in London. The second broadcast, on
Tuesday, was heard in Manchester, the third in Bristol, the
fourth in Blackpool, and I think the fifth was heard in Glasgow.
In those days you got a lot of mileage out of six minutes.

But what really amazed us was the number of people who
heard us on that one broadcast in London. And what was even
more pleasing, they all liked us. We may not have been
impressed with radio before these broadcasts, but we certainly
were afterwards. I couldn't wait to get back to New York. I
figured if they liked us in America as much as they did in
London, no telling how far Gracie and I could go in this new
thing called radio.

Now let's pause a minute. Before I take you back to
America, as long as I'm now in England, I'd like to stay here for
awhile and tell you what happened to me here in 1976. I know
you're just dying to find out how Gracie and I made out in
radio, but I'm sorry, you'll have to wait. I want the book to have
a little suspense.

Well, on June 13, 1976, I was invited to give a concert at the
London Palladium. It was a Royal Gala Charity Evening and
attended by Her Royal Highness Princess Margaret. It was a
very successful evening and raised a lot of money. At the finish
of my performance, Max Bygraves, one of the top English
comedians, presented me with a beautiful plaque. I thanked
him, and said, "It's an honor to receive this award, Max, and
when I get home I'm going to invite Douglas Fairbanks, Jr.,
over to see it, because he's the only Englishman in Hollywood I
know."

Following the concert, Jeffrey Kruger, who produced the show, ushered me up to the Royal Box to meet Princess Margaret. There were a number of people there, and seated in the center of the group was this charming lady. So I went up to her and said, "Your Highness, it's a pleasure for me to meet you. I'd curtsy, but if I got down, I wouldn't be able to get up again."

She laughed, and said, "I'm sorry, Mr. Burns, I'm not Princess Margaret, I'm the Lady-in-Waiting."

Just then the Princess came in. I turned to her and said, "Your Highness, it's a pleasure for me to meet you, and you just missed one of my big jokes."

The Princess gave me a puzzled look, and as she sat down she gestured for me to sit next to her. We had a very pleasant conversation, and then she said, "Mr. Burns, you sing so fast I practically missed the lyrics to your first song."

I said, "Your Highness, would you like to hear me sing it again?"

With a smile, she said, "No, once is enough." I had a funny comeback, but I'm not topping a princess.

Well, a few minutes later the Princess stood up, and I assumed that this was my cue to leave. As I said goodbye and started to go, she stopped me and whispered, "No, no, Mr. Burns, I'm supposed to leave first." I quickly stepped aside, and she left. Then as I started to leave again, the Lady-in-Waiting tapped me on the shoulder and said, "Mr. Burns, I'm supposed to leave next." After she left I sat down; I didn't want to start another war with England. I sat there until everybody had left. Finally an usher opened up the curtains to the box and said, "Mr. Burns, the theater is empty, and you can leave after I do."

Well, that's not exactly what happened. As a matter of fact, none of it is true. Oh, some of it is true. I might even say that most of it is true. I really did give the concert, I met Princess Margaret, and I was the last one to leave. That's because I curtsied and couldn't get up.

And now . . . back to the drama! This is how Gracie and I got into this new thing called radio. When we returned to New York from London we played a couple of weeks of vaudeville. About then Eddie Cantor and George Jessel were putting together a show to play the Palace Theater for a couple of weeks—I believe it was 1930—and they asked us to join it. We were thrilled because this was the tail end of vaudeville, and it looked like maybe there would be no more Palace. Anyway, the show was a smash and we stayed there for eleven weeks.

At that same time Eddie Cantor was also starring every Sunday night in radio on the *Chase and Sanborn Hour*, which was one of the top shows on the air. One day Eddie told me he'd like to use Gracie on his radio show. I said, "Sure, Eddie, we'd be delighted to do your show."

"I'm sorry, George," he said, "just Gracie."

"Okay, Eddie," I said, "under one condition. Providing you use our material."

"Fine, just write it up," Eddie nodded, "and I want Gracie to do about five minutes."

I said, "Eddie, there's nothing to write. All you say to Gracie is 'How's your brother?' and she'll talk for five minutes."

Eddie looked at me with those big eyes, and said, "That's all I do?"

"That's all I do," I said. "But if you feel like it, you can throw in some of my big ad libs like 'Really?' . . . 'Is that so.' . . . 'You don't say' . . . 'Oh?' . . . and 'Hmmmm.'"

So Gracie did the *Chase and Sanborn Hour* with Eddie Cantor and she was a very big hit. And that's how I got into radio.

The following week we were asked to do a guest spot on the *Rudy Vallee Fleischmann Hour* (remember, that's when I had the problem using the wrong reading glasses). After that we were booked to do two guest shots with Guy Lombardo. His show was called *Guy Lombardo and His Royal Canadians*, Thirty Minutes of the Sweetest Music This Side of Heaven. But our five minutes of comedy didn't dare interrupt the music. It was the first time we ever did our comedy routine with a musical background.

But they must have liked us, because we were booked for two more weeks. At the end of our third week, John Reber, who was then head of the Radio Department of the J. Walter Thompson Agency, got a letter signed by fifty-four members of an Ivy League college fraternity. He called me into his office and said, "George, sit down, I want to read this to you." I did, and then Reber read the following letter:

Gentlemen:

For the past two years every Monday night has been very special for us. It has become a tradition that on that night we invite our girlfriends over to the fraternity house and dance to the music of Guy Lombardo and His Royal Canadians, Thirty Minutes of the Sweetest Music This Side of Heaven. However, for the past three weeks out comes five minutes of these lousy jokes. May we point out that if we want lousy jokes, we can get them from the same joke book they get them from. Please, stick to the music, don't ruin our evening.

And then followed fifty-four signatures.

When he finished reading the letter, Reber looked up at me. I said, "John, I think you're trying to tell me something."

"That's right," he said. "George, anytime you can get fifty-four fellows to sign their names to a letter like that, you and Gracie must have something. You're booked for four more weeks."

I got up and said, "Thanks, John. I'm going out to buy another joke book."

In case you think that's the end of the story, it isn't. A couple of weeks later John Reber got another letter from the same fraternity. This time they said that after they were forced to listen to us they had learned to like us. But on this letter there were only fifty-three signatures; one kid still held out.

Well, we stayed with Guy Lombardo for the rest of the season, which was thirty-nine weeks. Our popularity kept growing and growing. Actually, we didn't realize how well known we'd become until one Sunday night after we had been on the air for about eight weeks, we went to the Club Richman. Every Sunday night there was celebrity night, and after Harry Richman entertained he would introduce all the celebrities who were in the audience. The night we were there, after all the introductions, Jay C. Flippen, the well-known monologist and a friend of ours, called Richman aside and said, "Harry, you forgot to introduce Burns and Allen."

Harry said, "Burns and Allen? What do the boys do?"

Flippen put his arm around Richman's shoulder. "It's George Burns and Gracie Allen. Harry, do me a favor, just introduce them." And Harry Richman did. With that the place came apart, we got the biggest reception of anybody there. But as I said before, we'll take some of the credit, but most of it goes to the fellow who invented the little talking box.

Eventually Guy Lombardo left the show and they asked us to take over. The following season it was *The George Burns and Gracie Allen Show,* and we stayed in radio for nineteen years.

SOME OF MY BEST IN-LAWS
WERE IRISH

Now I've told you a lot about my family, I think it's time to tell you a little about Gracie's family. They were Irish Catholic and lived in San Francisco. She had a brother named George, and three sisters, Bessie, Pearl, and Hazel. Gracie was the baby of the family. She was the youngest by seven years, and of course, her mother and father were the oldest. They were a close, happy family, and most of them were in show business. I never had the chance to meet Gracie's father, but she told me he was in vaudeville, but only played the West Coast. These acts who played just the West Coast were called "Coast Defenders." Why they were called Defenders I don't know, unless they had to defend themselves once in a while from the audience. Anyway, that's the best I can come up with.

Now here's the way Gracie described her father's act to me. He sang Irish songs, told stories, and did clog dancing. And for the finish of his act they would bring out this contraption consisting of four posts and a wooden ceiling attached to it. Hanging from the ceiling were two straps, and he would grab hold of the straps, turn himself upside down, and do a fast Irish jig on the ceiling. I think I was right about why they called them Defenders.

Gracie's mother was a tiny, charming little lady. Everybody loved her. Although she herself was never in show business, she was crazy about it and encouraged all of her children to go into it. And they did, with the exception of Gracie's brother, George. I once asked him, "George, how come all your sisters are in show business and you're not?"

He thought about this for a moment, then answered, "I guess I just came to the conclusion that I have no talent."

I said, "Well, I came to that same conclusion years ago and just ignored it."

Gracie's three sisters were the greatest Irish dancers in the San Francisco Bay area. They were continually hired to dance at the various fairs and social functions up and down the entire Pacific Coast. And in between they entered every Irish dancing contest they could find. And they always came home with medals, blue ribbons, trophies, and sometimes even money. The only reason Gracie wasn't with them was that she was still a little girl going to school.

Now at that time there was a very large Irish community in San Francisco, and they could all dance and loved it. And every time the Allen girls would learn a new step they would name it after the person who taught it to them. So when they were sitting on the cable car on their way to enter a contest, their conversation would go something like this: "We make our entrance by opening with a Fitzpatrick, then we'll do a Sullivan, and then into an O'Neil. And, Bessie, you'll do a Kelly with a Ryan twist. Then following that, Pearl, you'll do a fast Flannagan, and I'll do a gliding Sweeney. And for the finish we'll all do a triple Mahoney." Their dancing routines always looked fresh because every time they made an appearance they would change the names around.

Now these Irish contests were not easy. Granted, the performers' costumes and their cuteness and their personalities would influence the audience, but not the judges. The judges sat under the stage completely isolated from the performers and the audience. They judged entirely by listening to the taps. And these judges were old great Irish dancers, and if somebody so much as missed just one tap while doing a MacNamara he was out. So Gracie's sisters must have been fabulous Irish dancers. To win all those contests under those conditions they had to be.

These three girls were a riot. Hazel never stopped talking, Pearl never said a word, and Bessie never listened. It worked for Bessie. She never got involved, she never got into an argument, she couldn't be bothered—which reminds me of an old joke, about sixty years old. Now a sixty-year-old joke might be an old joke to you, but at my age a sixty-year-old joke is brand new. Anyway, joke:

> This married couple had her brother-in-law living with them for about five years. So Sam said to Sarah, "We've got to get rid of your brother Joe. At dinner tonight I'll say, 'the soup is hot,' you say, 'the soup is cold,' and if he agrees with me, I'll throw him out, and if he agrees with you, you throw him out."
>
> At dinner that night Sam said to Joe, "Is the soup hot or cold?" and Joe said, "I'm not answering, I'm staying five more years."

That was Bessie.

As I told you, Hazel loved to talk. She was a very outgoing, friendly person. She talked to people on the street, she talked to everybody. When she went to the market to buy some tomatoes, by the time she stopped talking to the grocer the tomatoes were out of season. She even went so far as to learn to speak Gaelic so she could talk to more people.

While Pearl was a fine Irish dancer, I don't think she loved it like her sisters did. In fact, I feel that she resented being a good dancer. Her sisters told me that Pearl wore out four pairs of dancing shoes to their one. I guess she was so angry she had talent that she took it out on the floor.

Once when the three Allen sisters were playing in Santa
Cruz we had one of our famous California earthquakes. While
nothing happened to the girls, Mrs. Allen up in San Francisco
didn't know that. All she knew was what she had heard on the
radio. She got all excited and ran to the neighbor next door. She
said, frightened, "Pearl, Bessie, and Hazel are in Santa Cruz,
and there's an earthquake there! What should I do?!"

The neighbor quipped, "Relax, they were a noisy bunch
anyway."

I don't think Mrs. Allen ever borrowed sugar from her
again.

Gracie told me another story about her mother that I think is
amusing and rather revealing. While Gracie was in school and
the other girls were on the road, Mrs. Allen was having her
living room repainted. And naturally she hired an Irish painter.
As he worked he sang *comailes*, what she called slow Irish
ballads. The problem was he painted in time to his singing.
Whenever he'd hold a long note he never moved the brush. It
went something like this:

'Twas on the thirty-first of August in the middle of
    July-y-y-y-y-y-y-y

And during July-y-y-y-y-y-y-y that brush didn't move for
twenty seconds. Then he'd continue singing.

The afternoon was wet and the mornin' it was
    dry-y-y-y-y-y-y
I met a fair young lady sittin' under an old oak
    tre-e-e-e-e-e
The divil a word I said to her-r-r-r-r-r-r
And the same she said to me-e-e-e-e-e-e!

After the third *comaile* Mrs. Allen walked into the room,
looked around, and said, "Look, John McCormack, if you insist

on singing while you're working, sing fast Irish jigs, and you might get the room done by Christmas."

The painter said, "But, Mrs. Allen, I don't know any fast Irish jigs."

"Very well," responded Mrs. Allen, "then you paint and I'll sing!" And sing she did. (I'm not sure, but I think Gracie's mother stole the bit from the Pee Wee Quartet.)

During this time Gracie was getting her education at The Star of the Sea Academy, a Catholic girls' school. Now Gracie's best friend was a girl she had grown up with. They did everything together and when they were about fourteen they were in the same class at the Academy. One day in art class the assignment was to draw whatever came to mind first. Gracie drew pictures of various stage costumes, but her girlfriend drew nothing but religious pictures. Right then and there one could see that these close friends were going in different directions. And they did. Gracie went into show business, and her friend stayed in the Church, became Sister Agnes and eventually a Mother Superior. Years later after Gracie and I were married we were making a movie at Paramount and Gracie invited Sister Agnes to come on the set and watch us. In between scenes I was sitting with the two of them, and I said, "Isn't it funny, Sister, you and Gracie were brought up together, but as close as you were you went in entirely opposite directions. You joined the Church, and Gracie went into show business. Just imagine, if that had been reversed, right now you'd be sleeping with me."

Gracie just fell apart with laughter, and so did Sister Agnes. That was one of my biggest laughs, and it was a novelty because at that time I was a dead-on straight man.

Well, Gracie couldn't wait to get started in show business. The ink was hardly dry on her diploma and there she was doing a single around the San Francisco area, with Mrs. Allen traveling with her. Naturally, her act consisted of Irish songs, Irish dances, and for the finish she did a dramatic recitation about a poor Irish waif lost on the moors of Ireland. It's too bad Barry Fitzgerald never saw her act; he would have loved it.

While Gracie was doing her act, the Allen Sisters were still dancing up and down the coast. But Gracie and her sisters never worked together until they met an actor named Larry Reilly. I'm not sure, but I think Larry Reilly was Irish. He was considered a headliner on the Pacific Coast vaudeville circuit, so when he asked Gracie and her sisters to join him they were delighted. It was a big break for them. The act was billed as "Larry Reilly & Co.," and below in small print was "Featuring the Allen Sisters." The act was so successful that they got an offer to play ten weeks in the East. Well, Bessie, Hazel, and Pearl wanted no part of this. They all had steady boyfriends in San Francisco, so they decided to stay right there and open a dancing school. But this was not for Gracie; she loved performing. So the girls opened their dancing school, and Gracie went back east with Larry Reilly. He replaced the Allen Sisters with an Irish bagpipe player and now called the act just "Larry Reilly & Co." I don't know how the girls felt about being replaced by a guy who blew into a bagpipe, but I guess they were in love, and when you're in love who notices things like that?

"Larry Reilly & Co." did very well back east until they were booked to play a split week at the Main Street Theater in Mechanicsville. When Gracie arrived at the theater she noticed that the billing was changed. Instead of "Larry Reilly & Co." it just read "Larry Reilly." She didn't say a word, but on the train back to New York she told Larry she was quitting the act for good, the reason being the billboard in front of the theater just read "Larry Reilly" and didn't even mention "& Co." She wound up her little speech by firmly stating, "Mr. Reilly, I'll never work with you again because I was humiliated, I didn't get billing!"

Larry tried to make amends, but this kid didn't know Gracie. When she said "No," she did *not* mean "maybe." It wasn't too good for Larry, but it worked out perfectly for me. Two weeks later I met Gracie, and we never had a billing problem for thirty-eight years.

As the years went by, every time Gracie and I played San Francisco there was always a big family reunion at the Allen house. By now there was not only the Allen family but a room full of in-laws. These occasions were always very festive with lots of fun, a lot of singing, a lot of dancing. . . . In fact, the next-door neighbor was right, they were a noisy bunch. I remember at one of these parties in came a Mr. Callahan. He must have been about ninety years old; they even had to help him sit down. He was one of the original judges of those Irish dance contests. Well, the evening was full of gaiety and laughter, but the height of the evening was when all the Allen girls got up and did some of their old routines. Right in the middle of all this excitement, Mr. Callahan said, "Will somebody help me up!" They did, and do you know he danced two fast choruses of an Irish hornpipe without missing a beat. Then he took out his pillbox, put a nitroglycerin tablet under his tongue, and said, "Will somebody sit me down?"

All of Gracie's sisters were happily married, but Bessie's husband stands out in my memory as the most unforgettable eccentric character I ever met. He was a large, heavy-set German named Ed Myers. He was a scientist, he was an archeologist, he was an inventor; in fact, there was no subject on which he was not an authority. The man was an absolute genius, but he never worked at it. Money meant nothing to him. When he and Bessie lived in Glendale—of course, I'm now going back at least fifty years—Ed invented a new process for separating gold from ore. I can't go into detail about how it worked because after all I'm a singer, but this machine was revolutionary. Now he sold one of these contraptions for $420. However, the only time he'd sell one was when he needed $420. One day a mine owner came to him and said, "Mr. Myers, I'd like to buy six of your machines." But Ed answered, "I don't need that kind of money. The next time I'm short I'll call you and sell you one."

I always looked forward to having dinner with Bessie and Ed because I'd always leave with something to think about. One night he was philosophizing and said, "Do you realize that the human body is the greatest machine ever created? Imagine, your stomach can digest the stomach of any other animal, but no matter how hungry you get, it won't eat itself." I was glad to hear that because it had been on my mind for a long time.

Some of Ed's statements were even simpler. One Sunday afternoon I was sitting in his yard and he was working on some blueprint. He looked up and said, "George, you know I have a formula for settling all the debts in the world."

With a statement like that, I could only say, "Good, let's hear it, it might come in handy at the Friars Club."

"This will work with any amount of money," Ed continued, "but to make it simple let's start with ten dollars. Now there are ten people, and they all owe each other ten dollars. The problem is to get the first ten dollars, so you bring them together and they each put up one dollar apiece. Then they give the ten dollars to the first man, he pays the ten dollars to the second man, he pays it to the third man, and so on until the ten dollars gets back to the first man. He returns a dollar to everyone, and they're all out of debt."

I nearly swallowed my cigar. Later that evening when we were having some coffee after dinner, suddenly Ed looked up and said, "Well, it's nine o'clock."

"What made you say that?" I asked.

"The window rattled," he answered. "There's a train that passes ten miles from here exactly at that time, and the vibration causes the window to rattle."

I looked at my watch and said, "Ed, the window's five minutes slow tonight."

I didn't really say that to Ed. I didn't think of it then. How do you like that, it took me fifty years to come up with that line.

There wasn't a weekend that went by that a group of prominent men weren't sitting around in Ed's backyard trying to pick his brains. But Ed was amazing. He gave away ideas that could have made him millions. One of those afternoons the conversation of the group got around to airplanes. And one airline executive was telling about this difficulty the airlines were having. It seemed that the ice and snow would collect on the wings of the planes, and this extra weight was giving them problems. Ed stopped drinking his beer long enough to say, "Invent a defroster"—and they did.

When Ed was about nineteen and going to college back in Kansas City word got around that he was a young genius. That year they were having the State Fair in Kansas City, and a local lumber company contacted Ed and asked him if he could invent something that they could feature in their exhibit. Ed said, "Sure," and two weeks later he came up with a machine where you put in lumber and out came wooden boxes. But it was so successful they couldn't use it. There were so many boxes you couldn't get into Kansas City.

When Alaska was being developed, the government had a problem with one of their mining projects. It was necessary to pump water over a steep mountain, but the machinery they had was inadequate. The government engineers couldn't seem to find a solution, and somehow the name of Ed Myers came up and the government sent for him. So Ed packed his long underwear, hopped on a boat, and sailed for Anchorage. When he got there the engineers came aboard to meet him. Ed's first question was, "What's your problem, boys?"

They answered with, "We have to get water over a high mountain, but the water is so heavy and the incline so steep that our machinery can't handle it."

Ed leaned back in his chair and casually said, "Boys, don't pump all that water at once. Break it up with air. Pump once water, and twice air." He had solved that problem without even unpacking his long underwear.

In spite of Ed's eccentricities his marriage with Bessie was a good one. They must have had something in common because they stayed married all their lives. Bessie met a lot of interesting people whom she enjoyed, even though she didn't know what they were talking about. She used to sit there weekend after weekend hoping that someday the conversation would get around to Irish dancing. But it never did. Of course, Bessie had one big advantage that other women didn't have. . . . She always knew when it was nine o'clock.

Well, that about takes care of the Allen family. I enjoyed writing about them, and it brought back a lot of pleasant memories. Even though I know you can't live in the past, it's nice to have one.

I NEVER LIKE TO APPLAUD ANYTHING THAT CAN'T APPLAUD BACK

THE TROUBLE WITH vacations is you've got to go someplace. And I've been every place I wanted to go. Being an old vaudevillian, I've spent practically all my life traveling. When I arrived somewhere I'd perform, and when I performed I got paid. I'm not sure, but I don't think I'd enjoy spending two weeks seeing all the lovely sights of Ronkonkoma, Long Island. I never was much for vacations because I figured why should I go someplace where I have to pay.

However, on our fourth wedding anniversary the only thing Gracie wanted was a trip to Paris. Being a perfect husband, I said yes and tried to book a week there. But they turned me down. At that time I was thirty-four years old and Maurice Chevalier was forty-two, and the biggest thing in Paris. They didn't want anybody to hurt his career, and they thought I would because Maurice Chevalier and I wore the same size straw hat.

But I have to admit that after thinking it over I got very excited about Gracie and me spending a week in Paris. And we couldn't wait to get to Billy LaHiff's Tavern on forty-eighth Street to tell all our vaudeville friends. That's where we actors gathered after the shows were over. I said to Gracie, "Wait till we tell them we're vacationing in Paris; it'll knock them off their seats."

That night sitting at our usual table, I waited for just the right moment, and then in my best throwaway delivery I quietly said, "Gracie and I are going to Paris." But nobody heard me. So I threw away my throwaway delivery and in a loud voice said, "Gracie and I are vacationing in Paris."

I got about the same reaction as if I'd said, "Gracie and I are going to play three days in Altoona." Jesse Block of Block & Sully said, "You'll love it. Eva and I have been to Paris three times," and then turned to the waiter and said, "I want my roast beef rare." And Jack Benny came up with, "You've got to stay at the George V Hotel. Ask for Monsieur Philippe and mention my name, you'll get a rate," and then to the same waiter, "Make mine rare, too."

I looked at Gracie and Gracie looked at me. But I don't give up easy. I tapped the water glass for attention, and everybody turned to me. "You didn't let me finish," I said. "After Paris we're going to Vienna."

The only one who was impressed was Gracie. Jack Pearl, who was sitting with his wife Winnie, said, "Winnie has relatives in Vienna; we've been there six or seven times." And then Mary Kelly piped up with, "The last time I was in Vienna I couldn't walk past this little sweet shop in Ludwigstrasse. Eating those Viennese chocolate I must have put on ten pounds." And then Jack Benny added this, "George, when you and Gracie are in Vienna you must take in the opera house. It's absolutely breathtaking. And the acoustics are fantastic. The symphony was performing, and there I was sitting in the third balcony and heard every little note."

I just sat there thinking to myself, that takes care of Paris and Vienna. So I leaned over, and confidently said, "Has anybody at the table been to Budapest?"

"Yeah," Tom Fitzpatrick said, "I've been there." And the

waiter said, "So have I. It's beautiful." Tom followed that bit of information with, "Why? Are you thinking of going?"

"Not us," I blurted out, "we're just passing through Budapest on our way to Russia."

That finally did it. There was a moment of complete silence; then everybody at the table started talking at the same time. They were all excited about our trip to Russia—except me. I knew I wasn't going to Russia—and I wasn't going to Budapest—or Vienna. I was going to Paris, and the only reason I was going there was I liked to be with Gracie. But everybody at the table started congratulating us, and Gracie was so thrilled with the news that she threw her arms around me and gave me a big kiss. That's when I knew I had gone too far, and I better do something about it in a hurry. I tapped the water glass again and said, "I have another announcement to make."

With that, Winnie Pearl tapped her water glass and said, "So have I. My wonderful husband just told me that I can go to Russia with you and Gracie."

Gracie clapped her hands and said, "Oh, that's marvelous, Winnie," and the two girls hugged each other. "Now I'll have somebody to talk to, because George doesn't speak Russian."

I just sat there numb while I heard Winnie Pearl say to Gracie, "I understand we can buy sable coats there cheap." That's when I canceled my dessert.

And in the middle of all this hubbub Jack Benny tapped his water glass and said, "George, didn't you have an announcement to make?"

I said, "Yes. I just wanted to say that Gracie and I wanted to invite Winnie Pearl to go to Russia with us."

Well, a week later Winnie, Gracie, and I were on the *Île de France* on our way to Paris. Naturally, when we arrived we went right to the George V Hotel and asked for Monsieur Philippe. I mentioned Jack Benny's name, and he said, "I never heard of him." Anyway, we checked in and that night we decided to go to a Russian restaurant. You see, there's an old show-business tradition: if you do a new show, you break it in in New Haven before you bring it into New York. So we thought we'd better do the same thing with our stomachs. We'd break in the Russian food in Paris, and if we liked it, we'd take our stomachs to Russia.

It was a beautiful Russian restaurant, but when we sat down I noticed the dinners cost fifteen dollars apiece. And believe me, in 1930 that was a fortune. So I said, "Girls, our dinner is going to be forty-five dollars without any tips. This place is too expensive for us." The girls agreed and started to order.

That's when the waiter asked, "Would you like to begin your dinner with a little caviar?"

I said, "Certainly we want a little caviar," and after he left I turned to the girls, "What a question . . . do we want to begin our dinner with a little caviar? . . . For fifteen dollars I not only want caviar, I want a suit with two pairs of pants to go with it."

I must admit the food was excellent, so we decided to take our stomachs with us to Russia—until the bill came. They had charged us four dollars apiece extra for the caviar. That meant that dinner had amounted to nineteen dollars each. And I'm not going to tell you how much it came to with the tips or I'll start to cry again.

From there, like all good tourists, we went to the Folies Bergères to see the world-famous nudes. In the middle of the show, with forty beautiful nude girls on the stage, Gracie leaned over to me and whispered, "George, it's a little shocking, isn't it?"

I whispered back, "Shocking! It's outrageous! I'll never eat there again!"

Well, we stayed in Paris for five days and we really had a wonderful time. Of course, the girls did some shopping, and then we went to all the places the tourist books tell you to go. We saw the Left Bank, the Right Bank, we went to the top of the Eiffel Tower, took a trip down the Seine, we visited the Notre Dame cathedral (naturally I looked around for Lon

Chaney), and we took a guided tour of the Louvre. When we got to the *Mona Lisa* the guide very reverently announced, "You are now in the presence of one of the world's greatest art treasures . . . the *Mona Lisa* with her famous smile."

I piped up with, "She wouldn't be smiling if she ate in that Russian restaurant." Needless to say, Gracie and Winnie pretended they didn't know me for the rest of the tour.

From Paris we took the Orient Express to Vienna. I must say I was terribly disappointed; nobody was murdered on the train. As we got off in Vienna I said, "Girls, shall we take a taxi, or shall we waltz to the hotel?" After I got my laugh we compromised and waltzed to the cab.

We checked in at the Imperial Hotel, and Vienna proved to be everything we had expected. It was very exciting; the rolls were soft, the chocolate was sweet, the drinking water was ice cold, the streets were paved, and the towels were fluffy. This might not sound exciting to you, but I'm hooked on fluffy towels.

We spent three days in Vienna, and again we did what every tourist does. However, the girls insisted that one night we go to the Opera House and see a Wagnerian opera. That was the last thing I wanted to do. I'd never been to an opera, and I had never even wanted to go to one. But I had to go because at that time Gracie was getting all the laughs. My kind of music was Louis Armstrong singing "Ain't Misbehavin'," or Pinky Tomlin doing "The Object of My Affection Can Change My Complexion from White to Rosy Red." Me going to an opera. I always thought Caruso was one of the Marx Brothers: Groucho, Chico, Harpo, and Caruso.

That night the girls put on their evening gowns and I got into my tuxedo and off we went. The Opera House was gorgeous, the place was packed, and the audience looked very elegant. The opera itself was something to look at; the set was spectacular, the cast was enormous, the costumes were lavish, and the singing was loud and in German. And would you believe that at one point I got to be the center of attraction? Well, I did. The prima donna was singing one of her arias and when she hit this high note I started to applaud. I thought it was the finish of her act. The audience was horrified and everybody glared at me. How was I supposed to know that she was going to sing another thirty-two bars. But from then on I couldn't make another mistake because Gracie held onto one of my hands and Winnie held onto the other. And this wasn't easy, because I wasn't sitting between them.

This opera went on for about two and a half hours, but the finish knocked me out. The same prima donna was up there singing with the tenor and she must have hit a bad note or something, because suddenly he got mad at her, pulled out a dagger, and started stabbing her. And believe me, there were plenty of places to stab; she must have weighed about three hundred pounds. Well, he kept stabbing, and she kept singing. She finally hit her last high note, collapsed and died. When she hit the floor my cigar popped out of my holder. I'm sure when she landed it would have registered 8.2 on the Richter scale. And after dying she took twelve curtain calls. Now that really confused me. I'm a vaudeville actor, and in vaudeville when you died you were canceled.

The next morning we took the train to Budapest and checked in at the Gellert Hotel. I was amazed to find out that Budapest is really two cities divided by the Danube River. Buda is on one side and Pest is on the other. This caused some confusion for me, because when we had lunch the waiter said, "Would you like some wienerschnitzel?" and I answered, "I'll take the wiener and give the girls the schnitzel." You see, I thought everything was divided in Budapest. But that didn't get a laugh because the waiter didn't understand what I said, and the girls did.

At the next table there was a very attractive woman with three darling little blonde girls. I overheard the mother say to them, "If you don't eat your goulash, you'll all grow up to be very naughty girls," and the oldest one said, "But ve vant to be naughty girls!" I'm not sure, but I think those three little dolls turned out to be the Gabor sisters.

One of the biggest attractions in Budapest was right in our hotel. On the first floor was this enormous swimming pool with some sort of a machine that actually made real waves. On one side of the pool there was a large cocktail lounge where you could sit and have a drink while watching the swimmers. It was quite a gathering spot for all the young people. So Winnie, Gracie, and I went down to have a drink and take a look. Well, I don't mind telling you it was quite a sight. The girls around the pool wore very skimpy little bathing suits, but what really shocked me was the men. They all wore these tight little trunks with nothing on underneath. I shouldn't say nothing, because that's what shocked me. There they were—wieners without the schnitzel. Naturally, I was embarrassed for the girls, so I suggested that we leave. Winnie looked at Gracie, Gracie looked at Winnie, then they both turned to me and Winnie said, "Leave! We haven't looked at the waves yet!" So while the girls were looking at the waves and giggling I turned my back to the pool and finished my drink.

Look, don't get the idea that everybody in Budapest was swimming. Those who weren't were playing violins. I've never seen so many violins. Every time we left the hotel some kid would follow us and play the violin. The only way to get rid of him was to tip him. Well, this must have happened about twenty or thirty times, and I'm not crazy about the violin because I always had to listen to this friend of mine from Waukegan, I forget his name. But I did find a way to stop these kids from following me. I bought an old empty violin case and every time I left the hotel I carried it under my arm. It not only stopped the kids, but I got an offer from the A. & P. Gypsies.

We also made a point to see the famous Budapest Circus. What was so different about this circus was that it had a story line to it, and all the performers had speaking parts. It was amazing. The acrobats, the jugglers, the wire walkers, trapeze artists, animal trainers, clowns—while they were doing their tricks they spoke lines that were all part of the plot. And all this was done with musical numbers.

Well, I was so impressed with the whole idea that after we got back to New York I happened to mention it to Billy Rose, who at that time was one of our top Broadway producers. He must have been impressed with what I told him because he left immediately for Budapest, saw the show, and took the same idea and produced a big musical circus called *Jumbo* at the Hippodrome.

Three months later I said to Billy, "*Jumbo* is making a fortune for you, isn't it?"

"It certainly is," he said.

"Aren't you glad I told you to go to Budapest?"

"That's right," he smiled, "it was your idea. And George, to show my appreciation the seats to see *Jumbo* are seven dollars and fifty cents, but I'm going to give you and Gracie the house seats." And then he added, "But it's only going to cost you five dollars apiece." He made about $2 million on the show and I saved five dollars. But it was nice, we both came out ahead.

How I got into this Billy Rose story I'll never know, but I better get back to Budapest, because if we're going to Russia, we have to pick up our trunks. And that's exactly what we did.

As we drew near the Russian border I didn't know what to expect. Remember, I didn't expect to go there in the first place. However, at the border our two theatrical trunks proved to be a sensation with the Russian customs officers. They had never seen anything like them. The trunks were a bright yellow with heavy brass trimmings, and when you stood them up they were about five feet high. And on the top of the trunk it read "George Burns and Gracie Allen" in big, bold black letters. One of the inspectors pointed to the lettering and asked, "What's that?"

I indicated Gracie and me, and told him it was us.

He turned around to the other inspectors and said, "They

make trunks." Then he added to me, "You do beautiful job."

"Thank you," I said, "you should see our suitcases."

Wait, as long as I took time out in Budapest to tell you about Billy Rose, I must hold up the Russian customs inspection long enough to tell you about these trunks. They were the famous H & M theatrical trunks. They were enormous and beautiful, and they were a status symbol. If you were in vaudeville and owned one, that meant you were playing the bigtime. (I hope you noticed that Gracie and I had two.) Now one side of Gracie's trunk alone could hold at least twenty-five dresses and two or three coats. And these all hung on hangers so they never got creased. You could pull out these hangers and easily select anything you wanted. At the bottom of that same side was a drawer that held a dozen pairs of shoes. On the other side was a complete chest of drawers, an ironing board with a place for the iron, a small safe, a built-in radio, a special drawer that converted into a writing desk, and a deep drawer at the bottom that held ladies' hats. That was the H & M trunk. It was so big that if you weren't booked in a theater, you could play in your trunk for two weeks.

Well, when I opened these trunks for inspection at the Russian border they were a smash. Within minutes there were forty or fifty people gathered around gaping in wonder. Of course, I don't know if they were gaping or not because I don't speak Russian, but I know they were impressed. I remember saying to Gracie and Winnie, "I hope we enjoy Russia as much as they're enjoying our trunks."

After the trunks and we passed inspection, we got on a train and left for Moscow. This was almost fifty years ago so I don't remember much about the train ride, but I suppose we did what everybody does on trains; we ate something and looked out the window. However, we did reach Moscow, and when we got out at the station I was disappointed again. I looked around and didn't see Borrah Minnevitch & His Harmonica Rascals.

We checked into the Grand Hotel and met Natasha, our

Intourist guide, who drove us around and showed us the city. I have to admit the three of us were amazed. We had just come from Paris, Vienna, Budapest, where everything was lively, gay, exciting, and colorful. Here in Moscow everything appeared so drab and gray and somber. And the people all looked so serious. They looked a lot like the audience I played to in Schenectady.

For the next couple of days we saw all the sights one is supposed to see in Moscow, and they proved to be very interesting. But what we were really looking forward to was the Bolshoi Ballet. As it happened they were on tour and we were terribly disappointed. However, Natasha got us tickets to a concert of Russian folk dancing and it was a very exciting evening. They were absolutely marvelous. I'll let you in on a little secret: The Russians dance better sitting down than we do standing up.

Oh, I forgot to mention one of the first things Natasha told us was that giving or receiving tips in Russia was not allowed. (What's-his-name from Waukegan would have loved it here.) Well, that night we ate dinner in the dining room of the hotel. The food was fair, the soup was lukewarm, and the service was slow. There was a little orchestra playing, and they must have found out we were Americans because in our honor they played one of our folk songs, "Barney Google and His Goo-Goo-Googly Eyes," which was very difficult to dance to. After dinner we paid the check, and out of force of habit I left a five-dollar tip on the table. Back in our room I suddenly realized what I had done. I said to the girls, "My God, I forgot what Natasha told me and left a five-dollar tip. I might wind up in Siberia!"

I spent a restless night, but nothing happened. However, the next night when we went down to dinner the service was fast, the food was good, the soup was hot, and Gracie and I danced to "Dardanella."

When we were leaving Moscow I said to Natasha, "I've got a

confession to make. I left someone a tip, and he took it."

"Well, he wasn't supposed to," she warned me, "and he could get into a lot of trouble."

"What would happen if I gave you a tip?" I asked.

She answered, "I wouldn't accept it. I, too, would get into a lot of trouble."

"How about a half dozen pairs of silk stockings?"

There was silence for about half a minute, then she whispered, "That I wouldn't mind getting in trouble for."

And that's what the girls gave her.

Oh, by the way, her name wasn't Natasha. It was really Elsie. But if I called her Elsie, it wouldn't sound Russian and that would have been a terrible letdown for you. And that's the last thing I would do to my readers.

Anyway, we took a train to the Polish border, changed to a German train, and spent three days traveling through Poland and Germany and wound up in Paris. A very funny thing happened to us going through Warsaw, but I don't tell Polish jokes.

But we did have a very strange experience on the train. For three days Winnie, Gracie, and I were the only ones traveling first class. We had this whole car to ourselves, but no service. Nobody cleaned our ashtrays, made up our beds, gave us clean towels; they completely ignored us. We would keep ringing the service bell and nobody would answer. I think it was because Hitler was just coming into power and it probably was beneath the porter's dignity to wait on anybody who wasn't a member of the super-race.

When we arrived in Paris we picked up our grips and started to leave our compartment. Suddenly there was our porter blocking the doorway. After three days we finally got to see what he looked like. And he looked very unfriendly, and very big. He growled, "You owe me five dollars apiece."

"For what?" I said.

"For service."

"We didn't get any service," I said, and moved toward the door.

Still blocking the doorway, he said, "You owe five dollars apiece for traveling first class."

Now I was standing in front of him with this heavy grip, and right behind me was Gracie, who was small but very Irish. She pushed my grip, and the corner of it banged him in a very tender spot, forcing superman to take a bow. And while he was bowing the three of us made a hasty exit, with me leading the way. I know that in case of danger it's supposed to be ladies first, but that doesn't count when you're a coward.

We were hurrying down the platform when Winnie suddenly exclaimed, "Wait! George, stop! I left my mink coat in the compartment on the train!"

"Go get it," I said, "I'll wait for you."

Gracie gave me a firm look and said, "George, go back and get Winnie's coat."

What could I do? Suddenly she makes me John Wayne. So I put on my glasses and slowly started back toward our car. Sure enough, there was the porter. But when he saw me coming he turned and ran the other way, he thought I was coming to get him. Well, when he ran, I ran, too. The faster I ran the faster he ran, only I ran right into the compartment, got Winnie's coat, and ran right back to the girls. This might not have made the history books, but it was the first American victory over the Nazis.

This was the end of our vacation, and an hour and a half later we were in Le Havre getting ready to board the *Île de France* for home. As we approached the gangplank a man in a trench coat, with his collar pulled up and his hat pulled down, came up to me and said, "Comrade Burns? I'm from Russian secret police. In Moscow you tipped waiter five dollars. That's against law." While I was putting on my glasses in case of trouble he handed me the five dollars and said, "Here, we don't take tips in Russia."

"How about a half dozen pairs of silk stockings?" I asked.

"That I'll take," he said.

That last story isn't true, but being the end of the chapter I thought it needed a little something.

FUNNY ROUTINES CAN HURT YOUR CAREER

In 1932 Gracie and I signed a two-year contract with Paramount to make feature pictures. So besides having our own weekly radio show, we were now going to be movie stars. The first thing we had to do was move to Hollywood. And the first mistake we made was to ask Gracie's sister Bessie to find a house for us. Remember, Bessie was the one who was married to Ed Myers who told time by the rattle of the window.

She not only found us a house, she found us an Italian villa on four and a half acres. It was so big we didn't have any next-door neighbors. It was located on Sunset Boulevard right in the middle of Beverly Hills. In fact, I had a chance to buy all that property for eighty thousand dollars, but I turned it down. When I was young I was a very shrewd businessman. I wasn't going to let them put anything over on me, so I leased it for two years.

What a place. The bird bath was so big you could drown in it. I guess it was for eagles. The regular pool was enormous. It was made of decorative Italian tile and marble, and it even had a bridge over it that was a replica of the Rialto Bridge in Venice. That pool came in handy because I wear water wings when I take a shower.

The house was huge with dozens of enormous rooms. Even the furniture was big and heavy. Every time Gracie wanted to sit in a chair I had to lift her up. We spent most of our time in the kitchen because that was the only room that didn't have an echo in it.

Of course, with a big house like that we needed plenty of help. I couldn't clean it; my back was always out from lifting Gracie. So we hired this husky couple. The butler was about six feet two with a big head of blond hair, and he never smiled. I'm not sure but I think he was the brother of the porter on that German train. His wife was no shrinking violet either. She looked like she could make a few yards on the football field. We also had a governess for our children, Ronnie and Sandy, an upstairs maid, and a gardener. But we did save a few dollars because the butler also doubled as the chauffeur.

Naturally we had to buy a big car. It was an extra-long, custom-built limousine with a glass partition between the driver and the passengers. We didn't buy this car to keep up with the Joneses; we got it to keep up with the house. But we had a problem with the car. The back seat was so deep that when Gracie sat down her feet didn't touch the floor. One day she said to me, "George, return the car and have them take six inches off the back seat."

I said, "Gracie, you can't do that. This car is designed by experts who get millions of dollars just to design back seats. This back seat is custom built."

"Well, mine isn't," she said.

There was a long pause, then I got very mad . . . because I hadn't thought of that line. But Gracie had won her point. We sent the car back and had six inches cut off the back seat. From then on Gracie was very comfortable, but when anyone else sat down on that seat they fell on the floor.

We were now living the life style of Hollywood movie stars. One day we were visited by Ben Blue, one of our top funnymen, and while I was showing him around the estate he suddenly stopped short. He pointed across the way, and in a voice that sounded very impressed he said, "George, you've got stables over there."

And very nonchalantly, like a movie star, I said, "Ben, would I live in a house without stables?"

Ben looked at me and said, "I didn't know you rode horses."

"Who rides horses, I just love stables," I added.

Now I'm glad Ben Blue noticed the stables, because I've got a very amusing story about him. Shortly before we came to Hollywood, Gracie and I took out a six-act vaudeville unit on a tour of eight weeks, and Ben Blue was one of the acts. We got a ten-thousand-dollar guarantee from each theater, out of which we paid each of the acts, and if the box office receipts were over a specified amount, the theater and Burns and Allen would split the difference. So if business was good we could make quite a bit of money.

We were doing four shows a day to capacity business, but we would do even better if we could just squeeze in an extra show. However, the only way that could be done was to cut Ben Blue's act from thirty-five minutes to thirteen minutes. And I'll tell you a little secret, it's very difficult to cut an actor, especially Ben Blue. Because as much as the audience loved Ben Blue's act, Ben Blue loved it even more. Now at that time I was paying Ben Blue $750 a week, so I called him into my dressing room and said, "Sit down . . . have a drink . . . here smoke a cigar. . . ."

"You can't cut my act," he cut in.

"Ben," I said, "now that you've brought it up let me tell you something. You're getting seven hundred fifty dollars a week and you're doing thirty-five minutes. If you cut your act down to thirteen minutes, we'll be able to do an extra show and I'll give you a thousand dollars a week. You'll be making two hundred fifty dollars a week more."

He stood up and indignantly said, "Who the hell do you think you're talking to? Thirteen minutes! That would mean I'd have to take out the 'Ten Cents a Dance' bit that I do with my wife, and that's the only thing she does in my act. If I cut that, she'd divorce me!"

I said, "Ben, forget it, I'm sorry I brought it up."

With that he stormed out of the room. I didn't even have time to powder my nose before he stuck his head back into the room and said, "Three hundred fifty dollars?"

"You got it," I said.

So we did five shows a day, Ben did thirteen minutes, and two weeks later his wife divorced him. Isn't that a good story? Aren't you glad that Ben Blue noticed my stables? But wait, there's more. His wife took him to court and sued him for six hundred dollars a month alimony. At the trial Ben defended himself. He said to the judge, "Your Honor, I can't afford to pay my wife six hundred dollars a month alimony. If I did that, I wouldn't have enough money to put gas in my Duesenberg."

The judge stared at him and said, "You've got a Duesenberg?"

There was a pause, then Ben quickly said, "But Your Honor, don't forget, I drive it myself."

The judge pounded his gavel and said, "The lady gets six hundred dollars a month alimony, and the case is dismissed!"

The moral of this story is if you can't afford a lawyer, you shouldn't drive a Duesenberg. Let's see, I didn't expect this story to go on so long. Now I've forgotten where I was living. Oh yeah, I remember, it's the house with the big bird bath.

Anyway, there we were, Gracie and I, anxiously awaiting the arrival of the script from Paramount. This was the script that was going to change our lives from vaudevillians and radio performers to actors. It was very exciting for me; I would never have to walk out again and say, "Gracie, how's your brother?" Well, the script finally arrived, and it was titled *The Big Broadcast*. It starred all the big radio personalities: Stuart Erwin, Bing Crosby, Burns and Allen, Kate Smith, The Mills Brothers, The Boswell Sisters, Cab Calloway and his Orchestra, and

a dozen others. The plot was very intriguing. It was all about
Stu Erwin and Bing Crosby fighting for control of this big radio
station. And on page 40 Gracie and I came in. It read, "Burns
and Allen now do four minutes of their stage routine," and then
we were not mentioned for sixty-five pages, and on page 105 it
read, "Burns and Allen do four more minutes of their stage
routine." That was our acting debut in feature pictures. We
were ashamed to use that big limousine we bought. From then
on whenever we went to Paramount we hired a taxi.

Well, we continued doing our weekly radio show while
waiting for our next movie script, and one day Eddie Suther-
land, one of Hollywood's top directors, rushed over to our
house. He was very enthusiastic and said, "George, I'm
directing your next picture. It's called 'International House,'
with W. C. Fields, Peggy Hopkins Joyce, Stu Erwin, and Bela
Lugosi . . . and there are two wonderful parts in it for you and
Gracie!" He went on to explain that I would be playing the
house physician in this large Oriental hotel, and Gracie would
play my nurse-receptionist. Then he said, "The story's full of
intrigue, and it'll be quite a challenge for you and Gracie, but
I'm sure you can handle it."

This was it. I'd be playing a doctor. I could see myself
wearing a beard like Paul Muni. I offered Eddie a drink and
asked him to tell me a little about the story. He said, "Well, the
plot is full of twists and turns, and Dr. George Burns and Nurse
Gracie Allen are right in the middle of them."

"Wait a minute," I said. "Why do we have to be Dr. George
Burns and Nurse Gracie Allen?"

He said, "Well, how else would you be able to do four or five
minutes of your stage routine?" With that I took back his drink,
showed him to the door, and as he left I tripped him.

Well, we did *International House*, and followed that with
*College Humor, Six of a Kind, We're Not Dressing, Many Happy
Returns, Love in Bloom, Here Comes Cookie, Big Broadcast of 1936,
Big Broadcast of 1937,* and *College Holiday.* And in every one of

those pictures we were always George Burns and Gracie Allen. All I got to say was, "Gracie, how's your brother?" I never had a chance to say, "Ladies and gentlemen of the jury, is this the face of a killer?"

   . . . or bang on the cell bars with my tin cup and yell, "Let me outta here!"

   . . . or "Follow me, boys, we'll head 'em off at the pass!"

   . . . or "Frankly, Scarlett, I don't give a damn!"

I don't know about the other lines, but I know I would have been great doing that last one.

SCREWBALLS, ODDBALLS, AND HIGHBALLS

You PROBABLY THINK because I ended that last chapter that you're finished with my movie career. I've got a 1 for you, you're not. While we were making all those movies some very amusing things happened that I'd like to tell you about. Well, they're amusing now, but they weren't all amusing then. They might not even be amusing now, but when you're a writer you write. Some of the stuff you write is good, and some of it is bad. I'd say that about 82 percent of what I write is bad, but don't go by me; I'm as bad a judge as I am a writer. Look, if it were all good, you'd be paying twice as much for this book. So relax, read it, and if you don't enjoy it, remember that you're saving money.

Gracie and I made a couple of pictures with W. C. Fields, who was one of the all-time greats, but he was not the easiest person to get close to. For weeks while we were making *International House* I'd come on the set every morning full of smiles and greet him with, "Good morning, Mr. Fields." He'd respond with a very small nod . . . about an inch and a half.

One day Bill Fields was doing a scene with Gracie where they were seated at a table in a restaurant. Gracie hit him with a very funny line, which I don't remember, and made an exit. That was the end of the scene, but Fields didn't like it. He felt he needed a line or a piece of business to top Gracie. So shooting stopped for about an hour or so while Fields, the director, and everybody else tried to think of something. Finally I went up to him and said, "Bill, I think I've got it. On the table you've got a glass of water, a cup of coffee, and a dry martini. When Gracie leaves, you take two pieces of sugar, drop them in the glass of water, stir the coffee, and drink the martini."

Fields was delighted. He said, "George, from now on I'll always say good morning to you . . . even if it isn't."

What he didn't know was that the piece of business I gave him was a switch on an old bit I did with Gracie many years before. During a restaurant scene Gracie hit me with a funny line and left. I then took out a cigar and my lighter, struck a match and lit the lighter, and with the lighter I lit my cigar. Then I threw the lighter and the cigar away and stuck the match in my mouth. That got a laugh when I did it with Gracie, it got a laugh with Fields, and it'll get just as big a laugh when I do it twenty years from now.

After that Bill and I became friends, and he came to our house for dinner once in a while. But the first time he came— (Wait, right here I'd better let you in on something. Bill Fields used to take a little drink now and then. And those now and thens were about five minutes apart. Whenever he was invited to anybody's home he always wore his vest, because in the pockets he carried four small bottles of gin. This was in case the host didn't have any . . . or enough.) So the first time he came to our house I said, "Bill, you don't need the vest, I've got all the gin you can drink."

He opened the front door, and in the typical Fields delivery, hollered out to his driver, "Clarence, my good man, take the vest. I'm getting my libation from another source."

As you know, Bill Fields had a very distinctive delivery, and there's a story about that which I heard in England years ago. It was told to me by Stan Stinelli of Stinelli and Douglas. It seems when Bill Fields first started in vaudeville he was a juggler. He juggled clubs and balls, and for the finish of his act he'd juggle cigar boxes. But he never said a word on the stage. Now his wife worked as an assistant in his act, and she was a very beautiful young girl. They were playing a London theater, and the star on the bill was a famous music hall comedian named Mike Donohue, who had a very funny way of speaking. The words seemed to slide out of the corner of his mouth. He spoke as though he were slightly tipsy. Anyway, Donohue made a play for Bill's wife, and she went for him, too. So when Bill came back to the United States he came alone. His wife stayed with Mike Donohue. But Bill figured that as long as Donohue could steal his wife, he could steal Donohue's delivery, and he did. Personally, I think Bill got the best of the deal. However, I'm not sure if this story is true, because Stinelli used to lie a lot.

Another big star around that time was Frank Fay. He was a vaudeville headliner, and eventually was a smash in the original Broadway production of *Harvey*. Frank Fay was one of the most talented comedians in show business. That was not just my opinion, it was also his. On stage he had class, poise, and a certain arrogant elegance. Offstage he was just plain mean. He hated everybody who was doing well. Why he hated me I'll never know.

I'll never forget when Gracie and I were just getting started and we played on the bill with him at B.F. Keith's Palace in Chicago. He was the star and the master of ceremonies, and at the end of our act he came out on the stage, ignored me completely, and started talking to Gracie. I was standing right between them, and he never even looked at me.

He said, "Miss Allen, I think that you're a great new talent. You're very pretty, you have taste, you have style, your comedy timing is impeccable, and I predict that someday you'll become a big star."

And Gracie said, "Thank you, Mr. Fay."

Then Fay leaned over to Gracie very confidentially, and Gracie, being a good actress, leaned towards him. There I was, practically hidden by those two faces. There was a long pause, and then in a loud stage whisper Fay said to Gracie, "But where did you get the man?"

Needless to say, "the man" was ready to kill himself. That wouldn't have been a novelty, I've died on the stage lots of times. After that every time I would run into Frank Fay he'd never say hello or goodbye, he'd just pass, and without looking at me he'd say, "Hold on to her."

But I finally found a way to get even with Fay. He always had lunch at the Hollywood Brown Derby and so did I. Now I knew he was a very devout Catholic, so I always arranged to sit in a booth near him. Just as his food arrived I'd go over to his booth and sit down next to him and say, "Frank, I just heard some sad news, Walter Catlett died."

Fay would put down his knife and fork, cross himself, and say a little prayer. Then just as he'd pick up his knife and fork again, I'd say, "And Tom Fitzpatrick passed away." Again he'd cross himself and say a little prayer. Then I told him, "Sam Bernard is not with us anymore." I kept on mentioning people who were dead until his food got cold, and then I'd leave. After two months of this he stopped eating at the Brown Derby. It was just in time, too, I was running out of dead people.

One of the stars that everybody loved and still do is Fred Astaire. And in 1937 when Gracie and I got an offer to appear in one of his pictures, *Damsel in Distress*, we were absolutely thrilled. But there was one little catch to it. Before we were signed to do an Astaire picture Fred had to approve our dancing. Now Gracie was a great dancer, so there was no problem with her, but "the man" was sort of a right-legged dancer. I could tap with my right foot, but my left foot wanted me to get into some other business.

But I wasn't going to lose a chance to work with Fred Astaire. After all, look what it did for Ginger Rogers. Anyway,

I remembered an act in vaudeville called Evans and Evans. They did a two-dance where they each used a whisk broom, and it always stopped the show. I figured if I could get Evans and Evans to come to California and teach us the dance, we'd do it for Fred Astaire and we would be in the picture.

Well, I located one Evans, but the other one had died. (Too bad I didn't know that when Frank Fay was still eating at the Brown Derby.) I made a deal with the living Evans to come out to the West Coast and teach us the dance, which he did. When the time came for us to audition for Fred Astaire we showed up with Evans, Gracie, and myself, my piano player, and three whisk brooms. We did the dance for him and Fred flipped over it. He said, "George, I'd love to do this dance with you and Gracie in the movie."

I looked at him and said, "Fred, it's yours." So instead of Fred Astaire teaching me how to dance, I taught him. And can I tell you something, he picked it up real fast; that boy's a pretty good dancer.

Well, the story I just told you about Fred Astaire had a nice finish, but now I'm going to tell you one about Judy Garland that didn't. It seems that I was asked to speak at a testimonial dinner given for one of the big stars in Hollywood, I forget who it was. It's hard to remember, because in Hollywood whenever there's a lull they give somebody a dinner. Anyway, at these dinners, before the dinner starts, all those who are going to sit on the dais wait together in a reception room until all the guests have been seated at the tables. This night I'm in the reception room sitting with Judy Garland, and Sid Luft, who Judy was married to at the time, took me aside and said, "George, you'll be sitting next to Judy on the dais, too, and you can do me a very, very big favor. Don't let her drink too much tonight because she has to sing."

I assured Sid I'd take care of it. When I went back to Judy there on the table were two dry martinis. I quickly drank half of mine, and when she wasn't looking I switched glasses. I did that in the reception room, and I did that when we were seated on the dais. I must have done it five or six times . . . maybe ten . . . I was so busy switching glasses I didn't have time to count.

About twenty olives later George Jessel, who was master of ceremonies, introduced me, saying, "Ladies and gentlemen, and now George Burns!"

I looked around and couldn't find him. Milton Berle, who was also on the dais, came over and picked me up. "That's you, you're George Burns," he said. I just stood there and started to make my speech without even going to the microphone. Naturally, nobody heard me, which is just as well since I wasn't making any sense. Milton quickly pushed me back into my seat, and Jessel explained to the audience, "George Burns' speech was written by that famous writing team of Haig & Haig."

Later Judy got up and sang "Over the Rainbow" and was a smash. She was over the rainbow, and I was under the table. On the way out after the dinner was over, Sid Luft said to me, "George, you were disgusting tonight."

Wait a minute, I'm getting away from movie making. My continuity isn't what it used to be. Neither is my . . . my . . . my . . . my skiing. Of course, Gracie and I were very excited about making movies, but I never thought there would come a time when we would ever try to get out of one. Well, it happened. I received this script from a producer, whose name I'm not going to mention. In fact, I'm not going to mention the studio, either. But our entrance into this picture had Gracie and me in a rowboat in the middle of the ocean trying to hitch a ride. Suddenly an iceberg appears in front of us and conveniently splits in the middle as I rowed through. It's true. I'm not going to tell you the rest of the plot because it's not as believable as the opening scene.

Now at that time I was handled by the William Morris office, and I told Abe Lastfogel, who was the head of the agency, that we didn't want to make the picture. So he set up an appointment with the producer, and Abe and I went to see him to try to get out of the contract. In a very nice way Abe told the producer, "You've got a fine script, it will make a funny musical and should make a lot of money. However, the parts just don't fit Burns and Allen, and they'd like to get out of it."

This producer, who had never done a picture before, and whose only claim to fame was he had written a couple of songs, looked at me and said, "Burns, have you got anything in your contract that says you have script approval?"

I shook my head, "No."

"Well, I have," he said, "and you and Gracie are staying in the picture. If I didn't think these parts were right for Burns and Allen, I wouldn't have had them written that way." He leaned back in his chair and stared at us.

Abe got up and said, "George, I guess the meeting is over. Let's go."

When we got out in the hall I said, "Abe, the meeting isn't over. Let's go back, I think I know how to get out of that contract." So in we went, and in a very nice calm tone I said, "Look, Mr. Producer, don't you like living in California? Aren't you happy out here?"

"Of course I am," he said curtly.

"Then why do you want us both to go back to New York where we came from?"

He raised an eyebrow. "Why would we go back to New York?" he asked.

Continuing in the same calm tone of voice, I said, "Because if we make this lousy picture, they'll run us out of town. This story is for Mickey Mouse. Gracie and I rowing through the middle of an iceberg . . . and W.C. Fields getting on a motorcycle that's able to fly to a golf course . . . you should be put away for okaying a script like that. This is your first picture and it's going to be your last. You'll be lucky if they let you write those crummy songs again."

There was silence for about a minute while I waited. I couldn't find Abe Lastfogel, he was hiding somewhere. Then the producer, his face slightly purple, got up from behind his desk, crossed over and opened the door. And in a voice barely able to control his anger, said, "Burns, nobody can talk to me that way and be in one of my movies!"

"Thank you," I said, and when we got out in the hall I said to Abe, "Now that's the way to get out of a contract."

But can I give you a little bit more. The movie was made, and it made a lot of money, which shows you how wrong Abe Lastfogel can be.

However, this was Hollywood, and I certainly was not one to hold a grudge. Two years later Gracie and I made a movie for that same producer. This was a musical, and the cast was made up of practically all the big radio personalities: Bing Crosby, Bob Hope, Edgar Bergen, Jack Benny, Burns and Allen, Martha Raye, Ben Blue, and also Betty Grable, Edward Everett Horton, Jackie Coogan, plus about thirty chorus girls. So you can see it was a very expensive movie.

Now this producer was making a play for the lead dancer in the chorus, so he was always on the set. He was producing, directing, rewriting, anything just to impress this beautiful girl. Well, one night we were shooting late, and at seven o'clock they brought in a catered dinner for the cast and crew. This gave our producer a chance to be alone with the girl, and he took her to a very chi-chi restaurant nearby. About eight o'clock we were all ready to go back to work, but there was no producer or lead dancer. About a quarter to nine they showed up. Have you any idea how much it cost the studio to keep a cast and crew that size sitting around doing nothing? And they were all on triple time. I don't know what the guy accomplished with the girl, but I don't think it was worth it.

Anyway, at nine o'clock the entire company was ready to shoot this big production number. But just as the camera started to roll the producer jumped up and hollered, "Cut!" and everything came to a halt. "I don't like the way the girls' legs look in white tights," he said. "Put them all in black tights "

"But we don't have any black tights," the wardrobe woman protested.

"Then dye these black!" he ordered. "I'm tired of making all these decisions!"

"Look, if you want black tights, we won't be able to shoot this until tomorrow," the director cautioned, "and this number will cost the studio a fortune."

Ignoring this, the producer said, "Wrap it up, boys, we'll shoot this in the morning." And then, just for the benefit of the lead dancer, he announced, "When I make a movie, money is no object." And then he left.

Crosby, Hope, Jack Benny, myself, Bergen, all of us, we just looked at each other. We couldn't believe what was happening that night. Finally, I said, "Look, don't underestimate our producer. Any man who can open a picture with Gracie and me rowing through an iceberg has to know what he's doing."

The next morning we shot the number, and all the girls wore black tights. The white tights looked better.

Well, there was another three days of shooting, which we completed in two weeks. The final scene was where Bob Hope and Martha Raye got married, and we're all down at the railroad station waving goodbye to them as they leave for Niagara Falls on their honeymoon. We all thought that was it until the producer said, "Wait, I just thought of a great ending. As the train pulls out, all you stars lock arms and walk into the camera."

For the first time I thought he made a little sense, until I noticed I was locking arms with Martha Raye, and next to her was Bob Hope. I went over to the producer and quietly pointed out, "Look, Bob and Martha can't be in the finish. They're not here, they're on the train to Niagara Falls."

"Don't be silly," he scoffed, "nobody's going to notice those little technicalities."

So we all locked arms and walked into the camera. That was the finish of the picture, the finish of the producer . . . and the finish of this chapter.

PLEASE PASS THE HOSTESS

OF COURSE, YOU'VE all heard about those famous Hollywood parties, so let me do a few minutes on them. Now that Gracie and I were working in the movies, we were invited to a lot of parties. One of the first big ones we went to was given by the head of Paramount Studio. It was an engagement party for Gary and Rocky Cooper. The invitation was for eight o'clock, so of course, we showed up at eight o'clock. I guess that's our vaudeville training. In vaudeville if you didn't show up on time, somebody sang your songs.

Well, we arrived at eight o'clock sharp, and as we drove through the gate we were greeted by five little barking dogs. One of the parking attendants took our car, a butler let us in, and there we were alone in this big living room that could hold at least 150 people. We were both served a martini, and I sat there looking at Gracie and she sat there looking at me. After about fifteen minutes of this I said to one of the butlers, "Where's the host?"

He answered, "Oh, he asked me to wake him at eight-thirty."

Ten minutes later Gracie, who never drank, started to feel

the effect of that martini. She left me, went into the powder room, put all the towels on the floor, and lay down and went to sleep. Now I was really alone, so I went outside and barked harmony with the dogs.

Eventually the guests arrived, and we had a fine time. Driving home that night, Gracie asked me, "Did you make any new friends?"

"Yeah," I said, "I met a cocker spaniel with a great sense of humor."

But that experience did teach us an important lesson about Hollywood parties: Don't arrive on time. The bigger the star, the later he gets there. In fact, we went to one party where Clark Gable was so late he never even showed up.

Our next party was at the James Masons. I told Gracie that the invitation was for eight o'clock, but we'd arrive at eight-thirty. We weren't big enough to show up at nine. When we arrived there, again, not a car. So I started to drive around the block. I said to Gracie, "We'll keep driving until about ten cars show up, then we'll go in." Well, we drove around that block until we both got dizzy, and at nine-thirty there were still no cars. Finally I said, "Let's skip the party and go home, I'm running out of gas." When we got home I phoned Pamela Mason. "Pamela," I said, "I'm sorry, but Gracie and I can't come to your party tonight, I've got a very bad headache."

She said, "Well, I hope it gets better by tomorrow, George, because that's when the party is."

Gracie and I stayed in Hollywood and made about seven or eight pictures in a row for Paramount. We finally were doing so well that we began showing up at parties at five minutes to eleven. But there was one party we went to that was a classic. I guess you could call it one of those "wild Hollywood" parties. Anyway, it was given by John P. Medbury. He was not only one of Hollywood's finest writers, but he had a mad sense of humor. The party was in honor of a comedy team named Olsen and Johnson who were experts in madness. They had a crazy vaudeville act, and also starred on Broadway in *Hellzapoppin'*.

There were a lot of things that happened at that party that I still haven't figured out. Medbury lived in a big house in the Hollywood Hills, and when you arrived you parked your car and walked about a hundred yards up a roadway to the house. Well, this night when we arrived there were no attendants to take your car, but instead there were four donkeys tied to a tree. So after we parked the car, we carefully stepped around the donkeys and headed toward the house. At the entrance to the roadway we had to go through a tent. Inside there was a man sitting on a toilet reading a newspaper. Without even looking up, he said, "Keep walking, you're heading in the right direction."

Well, we kept walking . . . fast. A little further on there was a man sitting in a big tree with a rifle. As we passed by he yelled, "This is private property, don't pick any of the oranges!"

By the time we recovered from this we were passing the garage. The door was open, and the interior had been converted into a gaudy bedroom. Over the door was a red light, and beneath it stood a sexy little girl soliciting business. In ten yards we had gone from private property to public property.

Finally we reached the house, and there to greet us was John Medbury and a charming lady whom he introduced as his wife. As I passed her she gave me a friendly little goose. And remember, this was in the 1930s when this gesture wasn't socially acceptable. As soon as we walked inside the butler came up to me and asked if he could borrow my matches. He said he had some candles to light. So I gave them to him. Later on I found out that he had done this to everyone. There were two hundred guests without matches. At first, this didn't seem to be a problem because there were plenty of matches lying around. However, they were trick matches, the minute you'd light them they'd go out. Wherever you looked there was somebody trying to light a cigarette. This was one of the things I couldn't figure out. The girl under the red light, that I understood.

Here are a few more highlights of the evening. The party took place in July, but there was a fully decorated Christmas tree with presents underneath it in the living room. And there was a big fat Santa Claus sitting there with a cane. Every time somebody would try to pick up a present Santa Claus would say, "Ho, ho, ho," and whack him with the cane.

Every half hour a kid dressed like a bellboy would walk through the room calling out, "It is now eight o'clock!" It was always eight o'clock, it never got any later.

The ladies' powder room was bugged, and anything that was said in there was heard on speakers placed all over the house. We heard one lady say, "What a stupid party, when the hell do we eat?" Then Medbury's voice came over the speakers, answering her, "We'll eat when I'm damned good and ready!" I never did find out whether Medbury was in the ladies' room or with us.

About ten o'clock at night Medbury introduced a Russian man who was dressed in full diplomatic attire complete with a red sash, and wearing more medals than Georgie Jessel. He got up and spoke for fifteen minutes in Russian and left.

Finally at eleven o'clock they served a beautiful and elegant sit-down dinner. About an hour and a half later in came a twelve-piece orchestra. They put up their music stands, took out their music and tuned up their instruments. After a few minutes of this the leader raised his baton, and the orchestra played a loud fanfare. With that Medbury stood up and proclaimed, "Ladies and gentlemen, the party's over." The musicians packed up their gear and left. And so did the guests. When Gracie and I went through the tent, the guy was still there, only now he was reading the morning paper.

Let's get out of Hollywood for a minute and jump to London. Actually, this story began in America, we jumped too soon. So I'm on a flight from Los Angeles to New York, and on the same plane was Anne Douglas, Kirk Douglas' wife, and she introduced me to a friend of hers, a very charming lady named

Olive Behrendt. We all laughed and talked on the flight and had a wonderful time. Now Mrs. Behrendt knew that I was recovering from open-heart surgery, and she asked me where I was stopping in New York. I told her the name of the hotel and that was that. The following day at my hotel I received a beautiful little gold pillbox. Of course, I wanted to thank her, but I didn't know how or where to get in touch with her.

Now we jump to London, and it's a year and a half later. I'm staying at the Inn-on-the-Park, and I'm walking through the lobby when who should I bump into but this charming friend of Anne Douglas. Naturally, I was delighted to see her, and this was my chance to repay her for the lovely gold pillbox she had given me in New York. We talked for a few minutes, and I told her I wanted to give a party for her and a dozen of her friends at Les Ambassadeurs. She said she wouldn't think of having me do a thing like that, but I insisted. I told her she would make me very unhappy if she didn't accept, so she finally gave in.

That Saturday night there were fourteen of us for dinner. I went for the whole bit, French wine, the works. Now Les Ambassadeurs is a private club, and the dinner did not come cheap. But the evening was a huge success, and as we were sipping our brandy I turned to our guest of honor and said to her, "You know, I never had a chance to thank you for that beautiful gold pillbox."

She looked blankly at me and said, "What pillbox?"

Never one to show my feelings, I took a puff on my cigar and blew the smoke out of my ears. "Don't you remember when we were on that plane together with your good friend Anne Douglas?" I asked.

"I don't know any Anne Douglas," she said.

"You don't. Then where did we meet?"

"Why I'm Mrs. Joe Fields," she smiled. "We've been neighbors for years, we live on the same block in Beverly Hills."

I sat there speechless. I couldn't do the cigar bit again because she had just seen it. Well, we all had a good laugh, and

Above, relaxing at home. NBC PHOTO
BY EARL ZIEGLER

Right, in the early radio days. TED
ALLEN

Left, four of a kind—clockwise, from left, Eddie Cantor, George Jessel, Jack Benny and George Burns. NBC PHOTO BY ELMER HOLLOWAY

Below, celebrating an anniversary with Harry von Zell. Gracie's the one in the middle.

Above, with Jack Benny.
JOSEPH JASGUR

Right, George and Gracie . . . oops! . . . Jack Benny incognito.

Above, CBS's William Paley pays tribute to two of his stars, Burns and Allen. From left, Gracie, Paley, George Jessel, George and Jack Benny.

Below, at a Friar's Club Frolic. From left, Dore Schary, Danny Kaye, Gracie, George and Eddie Cantor.

Above, in the early '40s. Standing, left to right, Benny Fields, Blossom Seely, Harry Ruby, George, Jesse Block, Mrs. Leo Spitz; seated, left to right, Eve Sully, Ida and Eddie Cantor, Gracie, and Al Jolson.

Below, in the early '50s. Eve Sully, George, Gracie and Jesse Block.

George and his team. *Above*, teaching his writers what makes people laugh. Left to right, Seamon Jacobs, Hal Goldman, Fred Fox and Lisa Miller. NATE CUTLER

Left, secretary Jack Langdon (at the typewriter) and manager Irving Fein. NATE CUTLER

Left, at Carnegie Hall during a "One Man Show."

Below, celebrating his 100th Birthday Party, a TV special. CBS PHOTO DIVISION

With Walter Matthau, *above*, and Johnny Carson and friend, *below*, on a TV special. CBS PHOTO DIVISION

Above, with Bob Hope on a TV special. CBS PHOTO DIVISION

Below, watching Don Rickles get a laugh on *The Tonight Show*, George joins Angie Dickinson, Carroll O'Connor, and host Frank Sinatra.

Above, Goldie Hawn. CBS PHOTO DIVISION

Left and *below*, Carol Channing. SEAWELL

Above left, Ann-Margret. *Above right*, Gladys Knight.

Below, Madeline Kahn. CBS PHOTO DIVISION

"Man of the Hour." George with Gene Kelly at the Dean Martin "roast."
NBC PHOTO

Above, George gets "made up" by Walter Matthau in *The Sunshine Boys,* 1975. M-G-M, INC.

Below, John Denver and . . . *Oh! God,* 1978. WARNER BROTHERS, INC.

Top, George steps out with the Bee Gees and Peter Frampton (second from left) in *Sgt. Pepper's Lonely Hearts Club Band*, 1977. DAVE FRIEDMAN PHOTO

Left, in a scene from *Sgt. Pepper's Lonely Hearts Club Band*, 1977. DAVE FRIEDMAN PHOTO

Above, with Brooke Shields on the set of *Just You and Me, Kid*, 1979. COLUMBIA PICTURES

Above, with Burl Ives in a scene from *Just You and Me, Kid*, 1979. COLUMBIA
PICTURES

Below, with the "No Shirt Gang" from *Just You and Me, Kid*, left to right,
Keye Luke, Leon Ames, Carl Ballantine and Ray Bolger, 1979. COLUMBIA
PICTURES

The newest George Burns hit movie from Warner Brothers, *Going in Style*. *Above*, counting the ill-gotten gains with Art Carney and Lee Strasberg. *Left*, contemplating a little mischief. HOLLY BOWER

when I got back to my room at the hotel I did what anybody would do who made a mistake like that; I killed myself. So, Olive Behrendt, if you happen to be reading this, thanks for that lovely gold pillbox, and I'm sorry that you missed the beautiful party I gave you in London.

Come to think of it, I gave another party that cost me a fortune and didn't pay off. My mistake that time was that I tried to make Jack Benny laugh. I should have known better. With Jack you couldn't try, it had to be spontaneous.

Anyway, here's what happened. One night I called up Jack and Mary and invited them to our house for a party, and I told them it was going to be formal. I hired six musicians and had a small dance floor put down in my living room. I also brought in two extra butlers for the occasion, and outside I had a parking attendant to park the cars. Well, at seven-thirty Jack and Mary arrived. She had on a beautiful evening gown and Jack was in his tuxedo. Gracie and I greeted them in our evening clothes, and while we were having drinks and hors d'oeuvres the orchestra played softly in the background. Around eight o'clock one of the butlers announced that dinner was served. Jack gave Mary a look and then turned to me and asked, "Where are the guests?"

"This is it," I said. "It's a party just for the four of us." Then I waited for Jack to fall on the floor and scream laughing. Nothing. He just kept staring at me.

Let me ask you readers something. If you were put in a situation like that, wouldn't you laugh? Of course, you would. But not Jack. Not only didn't he laugh, but he was very mad at me. He said, "You mean to say that you rented a dance floor, hired an orchestra, two butlers, and an attendant to park one car just to make me laugh?!" He took a breath and added, "You must be out of your mind."

"But Jack," I said, "you can dance with Mary, and I'll dance with Gracie. Then you dance with Gracie, and I'll dance with Mary. And there's nobody else here so they won't bump into us." Not a snicker from Jack, he just kept staring at me. So I thought this might do it. I said, "And Jack, if you're in the mood, you and I can dance together."

That did it. He got up and said, "Mary, let's go home," and they left. I'd never seen him so furious. When he got outside I heard him yell at the parking attendant, "Don't touch my car, I'll get it myself!"

Gracie was always the perfect wife. After they left she laughed and said, "George, don't feel bad, I still think it was a funny idea." Well, we had dinner, then I danced with Gracie, Gracie danced with me, she went to bed, I sang six songs with the orchestra, they went home, and I went to bed.

But that's not the end of the story. It seems that Jack went around telling everybody what an idiot I was to give him that kind of party, but they all laughed and thought it was very funny. I guess they must have convinced him, because weeks later one night after dinner the doorbell rang. I opened the door, and there was Jack standing there laughing his head off. He finally made it into the living room and fell on the floor still laughing. "Jack, what's so funny?" I asked him.

He gasped, "That party you gave me four weeks ago, that's the funniest thing that ever happened to me!"

I couldn't believe it. I leaned down and said, "Then why didn't you laugh four weeks ago?"

"Because four weeks ago it wasn't funny, now it's hysterical," and he continued laughing. I just stepped over him and went to bed.

Now there are some real wild Hollywood parties I could tell you about, but at the beginning of this chapter I told you I'd only do a few minutes on parties. I'm sorry, but the few minutes are up.

THANKS FOR LETTING US COME INTO YOUR LIVING ROOM

LET'S SEE, I told you about Gracie and me in vaudeville, about our radio days, and about our feature movie careers. Oh my goodness, I forgot that we were in television. Well, that's understandable, we were only in it for eight years.

Now for many radio shows, going into television was a big problem. They were afraid that people wouldn't like them if they didn't look the way they sounded. But for Gracie and me it was easy. Gracie looked even better than she sounded, and with me it didn't matter. Who cares how a straight man looks or sounds. My public couldn't be disappointed.

Well, when we went on television in 1950 we did make one adjustment. And it worked very well on our show. The executives at CBS had meeting after meeting trying to come up with all sorts of formats to give us a new look. I asked them why give us a new look when nobody had seen us before. I said, "Gentlemen, supposing Gracie and I do the same thing we were doing in radio, with one slight change. Gracie and I are still married, we have our next-door neighbors Mr. and Mrs. Morton, and the same kind of situations. However, I can step out of the set and talk directly into the camera.

163

This way I can further the plot, or complicate it, and make any kind of comment I want." And CBS bought this idea immediately.

I must admit that in the play *Our Town* they had a narrator who used the same technique. But I switched that bit completely. He didn't smoke a cigar and I did, so you can see that makes it entirely different. I'm full of those great switches. I just thought of another one: Happy Christmas and Merry New Year. See?

Our first fifty television shows were live. For those of you who don't remember, those live shows were not easy. There was no taping or filming ahead of time. While the actors were performing the audience was at home watching. When the show started, whatever was said or done, that's what went on the air. If a joke didn't get a laugh, it just lay there, there was no laugh track to help you out. And if you made a mistake, everybody watching saw it. I remember one actor walked out with his fly open. It didn't help our show any, but he got a lot of fan mail. My fly was open once, and not a letter. I told you nobody watches a straight man.

And there were other problems. The show had to come out on time to the second. If it looked as if a show was running long, the producer held up a sign reading "Talk Faster." If it was running short, he held up a sign reading "Talk Slower." One time Gracie and I were in the middle of a routine, and Gracie had just said, "When I cook roast beef I always put two roasts in the oven, a big one and a little one." And my next line was supposed to be, "Gracie, why did you put two roasts in the oven?" But just then the producer held up the "Talk Slower" sign. So I asked that same question something like this: "Gracie, let me ask you something . . . not that I'm inquisitive . . . and I know I shouldn't ask you this . . . but if I didn't ask you this, I couldn't sleep . . . not that it's important . . . but there's something I'd like to know . . . why . . . why . . . and please tell the truth . . . now why did you put . . . I mean why in the world did you put . . . not one . . . and not three—" About that time I looked up, and there was the producer holding up the "Talk Faster" sign. So, very fast I said, "Graciewhydidyouput-tworoastsintheoven?" And in the same tempo Gracie answered, "Whenthelittleroastburnsthebigoneisdone."

In those days we all had to memorize our lines. This was especially tough on Gracie because of the offbeat character she played. Her crazy answers didn't always go with the questions. For example, I'd say, "Gracie, how do you feel?" and she'd answer, "I'm glad you asked. My Uncle Harvey fell down a flight of stairs again."

So Gracie not only had to memorize her lines, she had to memorize everybody else's. I hope you're not confused, but what I'm trying to say is that normally when two actors are doing a scene if the dialogue doesn't make sense, they can't remember it. But with Gracie it was just the opposite, if it made sense, she couldn't remember it. Anyway, she memorized the entire script, and the only way she remembered her answers was when you asked the question.

Where I'm going with this is that on one of our live shows Bill Goodwin, our announcer, was doing a scene with Gracie. She was supposed to make a false exit, and he had a line, "Wait, Gracie, there's something else I have to tell you." But he forgot to say that line, so she kept walking right back into her dressing room and started taking off her makeup. She thought the show was over. I had to do something, so I took advantage of our new gimmick and stepped out of the set and began talking to the audience. "Ladies and gentlemen, in case you're confused, let me tell you what happened. Bill Goodwin was supposed to call Gracie back, but he forgot his line, so right now Gracie is down in her dressing room taking off her makeup. So you're never going to see the finish of the show, which I thought was very funny. But now that I think of it, what I'm doing now might be even funnier. Good night, everybody." Can I tell you something, what I did got a big laugh. They thought it really was the finish.

Live television was fun and it was exciting, but it was very demanding. After two years we were tickled to death when they started to put television shows on film. On film if an actor would blow a line, there was no panic, you'd simply do it over. There were no signs "Talk Fast" or "Talk Slow," it was all done in the editing room. Let's face it, on film the shows weren't always funny, but they always came out on time. Now I don't want you to get the idea that putting a half hour television show on film was a breeze. After all, that had its problems, too. Actually you were making a small movie every week.

I'll never forget when Freddie de Cordova was producing and directing the Burns and Allen Show (he's been Johnny Carson's producer for years). At that time Freddie was still a bachelor and living in a duplex with his mother. She had one apartment and he had the other, and he was a very thoughtful and devoted son. Now Freddie was a fine director, but he and I were always arguing about the show. Sometimes it would be about the opening, other times about the closing, or the way a line was read, or anything. And every time we would get in one of these arguments it would end with Freddie shouting, "This is my last show, I quit! I'm not showing up tomorrow!" So that night I'd send his mother two dozen roses, and the next morning, there was Freddie again. I kept Freddie's mother in fresh roses for about two years.

One day I walked into his office and said, "Freddie, I want to talk to you about the way you staged the finish of that party scene." As soon as I said that, Freddie started drumming his fingers on the desk and his face began to turn red. Before he could say anything I said, "Freddie, I just want you to know that I already sent your mother two dozen roses." We both looked at each other and burst out laughing. But there's a footnote to this story. Later on I found out that Freddie owned the flower shop.

Would you like to hear another Freddie de Cordova story? Of course you would. On one of our shows there was an actor who had only one line. He was supposed to come to the door of our house, ring the bell, and I would open the door and say, "Yes?" Then he'd say his line, "Hello, I'm Dr. J. J. Crothers," and I would say, "Come in." And that was the whole bit.

Well, Freddie had hired an actor he knew who hadn't worked for a long time. This poor guy was a nervous wreck. When it came time for him to do his one line he blew it. He not only blew it once, he blew it seventeen times. Finally, I called Freddie aside and said, "Freddie, this is ridiculous, we could kill a whole season with this one line. Let's bring in another actor."

"Please, George," Freddie said, "the man needs the job."

"Okay," I agreed, "but before we do the scene again I want to talk to him." I went over to the actor and asked him, "Before we try this scene again, what's your real name?"

"Philip Manchester," he stated.

"Great. Now forget that you're Dr. J. J. Crothers. When I open the door and say 'Yes?' you just say, 'Hello, I'm Dr. Philip Manchester.'"

The actor assured me, "No, no, Mr. Burns, I promise I can do it. When you come to the door and say 'Yes?' I'll say, 'Hello, I'm Dr. J. J. Crothers.'"

"No, no," I said, "I don't like Dr. J. J. Crothers. I wouldn't go to a doctor whose name was J. J. Crothers. In fact, when I get to the office in the morning I'm going to fire the writer who thought of that name."

"But please, Mr. Burns," he pleaded, "it's no problem. I can say it. 'Hello, I'm Dr. J. J. Crothers.'"

"Okay." And we did the scene again. I opened the door and said "Yes?" and the actor said, "Hello, I'm Dr. George Burns."

I said, "No, you're not. And you're not Dr. J. J. Crothers,

either. You're Philip Manchester, that's the name on the check you're going to pick up when you leave."

Well, the poor fellow looked so depressed and crestfallen that I couldn't go through with it. "Wait, I've got an idea," I told him. "We'll do it again. You just come to the door, I ask you a question, and all you have to do is say 'Yes.' Can you do that?"

"Yes," he said.

"That's a good reading, remember that," I added.

So we did the scene again. He came to the door and rang the bell. I opened the door and said, "Hello, aren't you Dr. J. J. Crothers?," he said, "Yes," and I said "Come in." And we did it in one take.

All the situation comedy shows had one thing in common; somebody was always eavesdropping, either listening at a door, peeking through a keyhole, looking through a window or whatever, so they could find out what was going on and plan their counterattack. Week after week I was spying on Gracie, and it was getting pretty monotonous. Well, one day my writers and I came up with a new idea that we were all excited about. We decided that we should put a television set in my den. That way, instead of eavesdropping I could just turn on the television set and tune in Gracie and see what nutty things she was up to. To us this was the greatest innovation since I discovered the wheel. But our sponsor didn't like it. He objected, "It's out of reality, you can't be watching your own show."

"Mr. Thompson," I argued, "we think it's a great refreshing idea, and I'm going to do it."

"Well, if you do, you might have to find a new sponsor."

"Then I'll just have to turn in my new television set and find one," I stated.

We finally compromised and did it my way, and it turned out to be one of the highlights of my show. Now this device is being used in banks, hotels, department stores, all over. I turned out to be the father of closed circuit television. So you see, I'm not only an actor, a singer, a dancer, an author, a producer, and a director . . . I'm also an inventor.

As you know, situation comedies can go on for years and years, and in that time the audience gets very attached to the same characters. The Burns and Allen show was on for about eight years and we had five principal actors. There were Gracie and myself, Harry Von Zell, and our next-door neighbors Blanche and Harry Morton, played by Bea Benadaret and Fred Clark. The chemistry between the five of us was like magic, right from the opening show the audiences loved us. We were a very happy unit. Now back in 1953 there weren't so many television sets in use, so naturally they weren't paying the kind of salaries they do today. Anyway, when our option was picked up for the second season I gave everybody a two-hundred-dollar-a-week raise, which was considered very generous. Well, after we finished filming the second show of the new season Fred Clark came to my office and announced, "George, with that raise you gave me I'm now making a thousand dollars a week, but it's not enough. If you want me to stay, you'll have to pay me fifteen hundred."

"Fred," I said, "I think you're a fine actor, but if I paid you that, you'd be making a hundred dollars a week more than I am."

"I'm sorry, George, but that's it. That's what I want."

I said, "You realize, of course, that I've got a contract with you for another year." He just stared at me and I continued, "But I imagine if I held you to it, I'd have a very unhappy actor on my hands . . . an actor who on the day of the show just might get a bad case of laryngitis."

"Oh yeah," he said, "in fact, just talking about it my throat is tightening up."

"Well, your throat might be tightening up, but not as much as my wallet. Goodbye, Fred, and lots of luck on your next job." I don't think Fred expected it to turn out that way. I was sorry to lose him, but there just wasn't that kind of money around.

Well, it was panic time. Here we had a hit show and we had lost one of our main characters. The network, the advertising agency, the sponsor, none of them knew what to do. We all had a series of emergency meetings trying to come up with an idea of how to explain the sudden disappearance of our neighbor, Harry Morton. Some of the solutions they came up with were beauties, especially for a comedy show; like Harry falling to his death from an airplane—or drowning in a swimming pool—choking on a piece of steak (that suggestion got quite a few votes)—running away from his wife with another woman. . . . There were others, but I've just mentioned the good ones.

We went round and round and got no place. Finally I said, "Gentlemen, I've got an idea!" and this is how the problem was solved. On our next show the story line had Harry Morton buy his wife Blanche an iron deer for the front lawn. Well, she hated it, and she was standing at the door with a rolling pin held over her head ready to slug him as soon as he came into the house. At that point I walked into the picture and said, "Blanche, hold it, don't move," and she froze in that position while I talked directly to the audience. "Ladies and gentlemen," I said, "Fred Clark, the actor who has been playing the part of Harry Morton won't be with us anymore. I gave him a two-hundred-dollar-a-week raise, but he was very unhappy and wanted five hundred dollars a week more. I couldn't afford it, so I brought in a very fine actor, Larry Keating, who is now going to play that part."

Then I turned to Blanche, and said, "Blanche, put the rolling pin down and come over here." Then I brought out Larry Keating. I said, "Larry, this is Bea Benadaret . . . and Bea, this is Larry Keating. From now on you're going to be husband and wife."

They both started complimenting each other saying what great performers each thought the other was, etc., and I said, "Okay, that's enough compliments, let's get on with the show."

Bea went back to the door, held up the rolling pin, Larry made his entrance, she hit him over the head, and a new Harry Morton was christened. And it worked. Everybody accepted the new husband, and I never got one letter asking what happened to Fred Clark. The sponsor, the network, and the advertising agency were all delighted the way it turned out. In fact, it worked so well I almost fired Harry Von Zell.

Oh yes, when it came to money I always made the right decisions. I remember way back in radio I was offered Frank Sinatra for $250 a week, and at the same time I was offered a singing group, two boys and a girl called The Smoothies, for $250 a week. Well, I'm not stupid, I figured I could get three for the price of one, so there was no question, I took The Smoothies. And I certainly didn't make a mistake, because all of you know where The Smoothies are today.

Well, our television cast with Larry Keating stayed together for seven years until Gracie retired. The only major addition during that time was when my son, Ronnie, joined the show. My daughter, Sandy, also did a few commercials. But I thought Ronnie could have made it in show business. He had a nice relaxed manner, he was tall and good-looking and had all the instincts of a good actor. I even offered to send him to New York to study under Lee Strasberg at The Actors Studio, where some of our biggest stars came from. But Ronnie turned it down; he said he would miss all the girls at the Luau Restaurant.

I said to him, "Ronnie, they have restaurants in New York that also have pretty girls. And the pretty girls in New York have the same thing that the pretty girls have in California, and in the exact same spot." He appreciated this lesson in sex education. In fact, he called that night to thank me from the Luau.

But I never did quite understand why Ronnie wasn't in love with show business. On our show I always made sure he had good lines so he got big laughs, and every week there was a different actress playing his girlfriend. And they were all beautiful. Among them were Carla Borelli, Yvonne Lime, Adele Jergens, Suzanne Pleshette, Raquel Welch, Mary Tyler Moore—but Ronnie still liked the Luau. So, there was only one thing left for me to do, check out the Luau. And I did. I went there one night, and I must admit that the Luau did have something special—the noodles in the chow mein were really crisp.

One of the things I missed most after Gracie retired was the double routine she and I did at the end of each show. It had nothing to do with the plot, it was just sort of an afterpiece. Here's one I picked out at random, and I hope you enjoy it as much as we did:

GEORGE

Well, Gracie, any news from home?

GRACIE

Yes. I got a letter from my little niece, Jean.

GEORGE

What did she say?

GRACIE

She didn't say anything. She didn't phone. It was a letter, and she wrote it.

GEORGE

I mean what did she write?

GRACIE

It's Spring again, and my family is putting on a backyard circus, just like we did when I was a kid.

GEORGE

Every Spring you kids used to put on your own circus?

GRACIE

Yes. Of course, admission was free, but that was only for people who could afford it.

GEORGE

Well, that's because we're living in a democracy.

GRACIE

Oh yes, isn't it nice. . . . Anyway, my Cousin Barney was the sword swallower, and what a performance he put on. The kids would cheer when he put a sword four feet long down his throat.

GEORGE

Could Barney really swallow a sword?

GRACIE

Oh, George, don't be silly, it was a trick. You know the scabbard that the sword fits into?

GEORGE

Yeah.

GRACIE

Well, before the show he would stick that down his throat.

GEORGE

I see.

GRACIE

Then when he'd slip the sword into it . . . .

GEORGE JOINING GRACIE

. . . everybody thought he was swallowing it.

GRACIE

Yeah.

GEORGE

It's a shame to fool the public like that.

GRACIE

But the admission was free.

GEORGE

Oh, I forgot.

GRACIE

And Uncle Otis was the strong man. He'd come out in a leopard skin and put big nails in his mouth and twist them between his teeth until they'd bend.

GEORGE

That's quite a trick.

GRACIE

Yes, but he looked pretty ridiculous walking around with all those bent teeth.

GEORGE

Well, they'd come in handy if he happened to get a crooked ear of corn.

GRACIE

Oh, you live and learn. . . . And Aunt Gertrude was the snake charmer.

GEORGE

Aunt Gertrude? The one who's so near-sighted?

GRACIE

Yes. She had a little snake and she was supposed to put it in a basket and then blow on a flute until the snake stuck its head up. And what do you suppose happened one Saturday afternoon?

GEORGE

She put the flute in the basket and blew on the snake.

GRACIE

Wasn't that awful!

GEORGE

That must have upset her.

GRACIE

Oh, George, it wasn't a real snake. It was just a few worms tied together.

GEORGE

Well, that's better. Who else was in the side show?

GRACIE

One of the big hits was Uncle Harvey and Aunt Clara.

GEORGE

What was their act?

GRACIE

Half man . . . half woman.

GEORGE

But didn't you have two halves left over?

GRACIE

Oh no, they both got into one costume.

GEORGE

Now I get the picture.

GRACIE

George, it wasn't a picture, they did it in person.

GEORGE

What was your part in the circus?

GRACIE

I was the lion tamer.

GEORGE

You were the lion tamer?

GRACIE

Of course I just used our house cat. For two weeks before the circus I taught her all kinds of tricks . . . to sit on a pedestal, to roll over, to play dead.

GEORGE

Sounds like a pretty smart cat.

GRACIE

Yes, but when she got in front of the audience she forgot all her tricks and just had kittens.

GEORGE

That must have caused a sensation.

GRACIE

It was . . . but what good was it? The silly cat wouldn't do it again for the second performance.

GEORGE

Say good night, Gracie.

GRACIE

Good night, Gracie.

You know, that was quite a while ago. I still miss those routines, and I always will.

A 79-YEAR-OLD STAR IS BORN

I HOPE THE title of this chapter doesn't make you think I'm egotistical calling myself a star, but I can't help it. That's what it says on my stationery. But it is true, I was seventy-nine years old when they asked me to play the part of Al Lewis in *The Sunshine Boys*. And it did start a whole new career for me. I'm not going to tell the story of how I got the part because I must have told it a thousand times. But if you haven't heard it, buy my last book, *Living It Up*, it's on page 213. Don't read just that page, read the whole book; it's very informative.

But there is one thing that happened as a result of *The Sunshine Boys* that I will mention again. I won an Oscar for the Best Supporting Actor. After being a straight man for sixty years I thought becoming an award-winning actor would change everything. But nothing changed. The following day I went to the Hillcrest Country Club and had lunch with Milton Berle. He looked just the same to me. And there was Georgie Jessel wearing the same medals. When I ordered matzos, eggs, and onions they tasted the same as they did when I was a straight man. Incidentally, there's a reason why I always order matzos, eggs, and onions. They sound like the name of a vaudeville act.

And for the same reason I order finn 'n haddie. I worked with them. Finn stole one of my orchestrations.

Anyway, that award changed nothing. I still get up at eight o'clock, I still brush my teeth with my right hand (sometimes I use a brush), I still do my same morning exercises, I still drive the same car, I still live in the same house, I still put my coat on with my right hand and put my hair on with my left. So you see, everything is exactly the same except for one thing—my stationery.

After *The Sunshine Boys* I got a few movie offers, but the one that amazed me was when Warner Brothers wanted me to play God in a new film they were making. And they weren't kidding. They had a script called *Oh God!* by Larry Gelbart, produced by Jerry Weintraub, directed by Carl Reiner, and starring John Denver and myself. It sounded very exciting, these were all very talented people. But after I accepted, I started to worry. I asked myself what am I doing? What am I doing playing God? How do you play God? What does God look like? So I looked in the mirror, and I didn't look like God, I looked like Al Lewis in *The Sunshine Boys.*" I was very confused, so I looked up and hollered, "How do you play God?!" But there was no answer.

I sat down and thought to myself, "Why would they pick me to play God?" Then I realized it made a little sense. I was the closest one to His age. Since Moses wasn't around, I suppose I was next in line.

The whole thing really bothered me. If I played Him, what would be my attitude? What would be my motivation? Should I play Him tall, should I play Him short? What kind of voice should I use? Could I handle a role like this? I finally called my manager Irving Fein, and said, "Irving, maybe I'm making a mistake playing God."

"How can you make a mistake?" Irving replied. "They're paying you a fortune. If there's anybody who might be making a mistake, it's Warner Brothers," and he hung up. Now during my career I've had a number of managers, but in all fairness to

Irving I must pay him a compliment. Nobody can hang up a phone like he does.

However, I still needed help, so I turned to some of my actor friends. First, I went to Jimmy Stewart and asked him how he thought I should play God. He thought a second, and then he said, "Well . . . uh . . . well, uh . . . George, you . . . you . . . see, if . . . if . . . I . . . I . . . were you, I'd . . . I'd . . . play him . . . uh . . . slow . . . uh . . . uh . . . relaxed . . . uh . . . uh . . . uh . . . soft, easy and . . . and . . . whatever you do, don't . . . uh, don't . . . uh, don't rush it." All I know is if God worked as slow as that, He never could have created the earth in six days. He'd still be at it.

I talked to Lucille Ball next. "Lucy," I said, "you're a fine actress, and I've got a problem and need your help. How should I play God?"

She answered, "If I were you, George, I'd play her very motherly."

After that I turned to one of the top actors in our industry, Orson Welles. "Orson," I asked, "if you played God, how would you play him?"

"Sitting down," was his answer.

So far I wasn't getting very far. If I took the advice I had received, my God would be a very slow mother sitting down. But then I got an inspiration. There was one person who could impersonate anybody. Rich Little. So I asked him, "I'm playing God, Rich. What kind of voice should I use?

"That's simple," he said, and he did a voice for me.

I said, "Rich, that sounds like Danny Thomas."

"That's right," he said, "God stole his delivery."

Well, everyone had a different idea, so I finally turned to the one man who could tell me how to do it—me. I used all my own instincts and played Him as honestly as I could. And it worked. It had to work. I couldn't be criticized. Nobody has ever seen Him, so they didn't know whether I was good or bad.

We finally started shooting the movie, and John Denver was

a delight to work with. It was his first movie and he turned out to be an excellent actor. In one of our early scenes he asks me to perform a miracle to prove to him that I'm God. What he didn't realize was that the real miracle was that I was able to get to the studio every morning.

We all worked together easily, but every once in a while Carl Reiner would have an objection to my interpretation of the role. He'd take me aside and say, "Look, George, this scene isn't moving, it needs a little more God-stuff." Another time he said, "George, we're going to do that scene over, it needs more Goddishness." Once he stopped a scene right in the middle by saying, "Hold it! George, you read that speech all wrong. God would never say it that way."

"Look, Carl," I said, "the last time you had lunch with Him did He have any other suggestions?"

Carl paused for a second, then started to laugh. "Okay, George, do it your way."

Carl Reiner and I had a very delightful relationship. One day just before lunch he came up to me a little worried and said, "George, I'm in trouble. I'm supposed to speak at a luncheon today at the Sportsmen's Lodge, and I forgot my toupee. Can I borrow yours?"

"Of course, Carl, what are friends for?" So he put on my toupee and left. When he returned I asked him, "How did your speech go, Carl?"

"Your hair was a riot," he said.

Now when I play a role I really throw myself into it. I've always been that way. Even in small-time vaudeville, doing bad acts in broken-down theaters, when I walked on the stage I threw myself into the part. Sometimes the manager would take a look at me and throw me out. I remember one theater they threw me out before I had a chance to throw myself in.

But now that I'm an actor I really live the part. Before they started shooting *Oh God!* I rehearsed day and night. I rehearsed when I was driving my car, I rehearsed before dinner, I rehearsed after dinner, I rehearsed while I was doing my exercises, I never stopped. I finally got so carried away rehearsing the part that one night before I went to bed when I said my prayers, I realized I was talking to myself.

The next morning, to stay in the mood, when I came downstairs to breakfast I wore a flowing white robe and sandals. I ran into Daniel, the man who works for me, and gave him a long list of things I wanted done that day. He waited patiently until I was all through, and then said, "Mr. Burns, you may be God at the studio, but this is Thursday, my day off." That day God had to take his car to the gas station all by himself.

Well, the movie came out and was a tremendous hit. It made millions of dollars. I guess the reason for that was that John Denver attracted all his fans, and I brought in the kids. That's not true, it's just a little joke. Well, it's not exactly a little joke, it's a tiny joke. It's not even that, it's no joke. In fact, if it weren't already printed, I'd take it back.

Truthfully, in my opinion, the real reason the picture was such a big hit was the casting of John Denver. He was the perfect one for the part. He practically played himself; a kind, considerate, honest man who was concerned not only about his fellow man, but every living thing. If God actually came down to talk to one good man, it could have been John Denver. I don't think the picture would have worked if I had come down and talked to Milton Berle. Not that Milton isn't a good man, but he'd be standing there with a pad and pencil taking down all my good stuff. I wouldn't have enjoyed that. Besides, I don't think it would be believable to have Milton Berle jot down "Thou Shalt Not Steal."

After the movie had been out a couple of months I got hundreds of letters just addressed to "God," and they'd be delivered to my house. When I went to a restaurant, the maître d' would ask, "Where would God like to sit?" The cocktail waitress would come over and say, "Would God like it with one olive or two?" Even strangers on the street would wave to me and say, "Have a nice day, God!" It was great for my ego but did nothing for my sex life.

To this day people still keep asking me, "Was there a message in the picture?" There certainly was, and this is it: If you make a lot of money for Warner Brothers, you'll continue making pictures for them. And it's true, I am doing several more for them which I'll talk about later.

After the picture with John Denver I played a cameo role in *Sergeant Pepper's Lonely Hearts Club Band.* What a shock it was for me to go from *The Sunshine Boys* and *Oh God!*, two nice warm intimate movies, to this raucous rock musical. When I walked on the set I couldn't believe my eyes. They had built an entire town called Heartland, U.S.A., that cost $750,000. I played in towns like Altoona that didn't cost that much.

The cast was loaded with all the high-priced young rock stars, and instead of dressing rooms every one of them was furnished with a luxurious motor home. Now I'd seen a plush motor home before, but I'd never seen forty of them lined up in a row. It looked like a millionaire's Leisure World. These homes had everything; a wet bar, a complete kitchen, tub and shower, a television set, everything but a swimming pool. The refrigerator was stocked with gourmet delicacies of every kind, and the liquor cabinet looked like the wine cellar of the 21 Club. After spending the first day in my motor home, when I went back to my Beverly Hills house and looked around I got the impression I wasn't doing well. In fact, I sent my butler out for food stamps.

The first day I was on the set, aside from the expensive cast and the large crew, there were 30 dancers and 450 extras. I have no idea what this picture cost Robert Stigwood, the producer, but I hope his mother and father are very rich. And if they were rich, they're not anymore.

It was a new world for me, working with all these kids. There were The BeeGees, Peter Frampton, Aerosmith, and then there was a group whose name sounded like a weather report. What was it again? Oh, yeah, Earth, Wind and Fire. And then there was— Wait, I've got to stop and tell you about Peter Frampton. I was talking to his manager, while we were sitting in the foyer of my motor home, and he told me that the year before when Peter was twenty-four years old, that little kid made $52 million. I was so shocked I nearly fell out of my Louis XIV rocking chair. Then his manager told me how he made it. That year Peter Frampton made one album that sold sixteen million copies, from which he received $3.00 each. Right there you've got $48 million. The other $4 million he made playing concerts.

Twenty-four years old . . . $52 million . . . I couldn't get over it. As soon as I was alone I called Irving Fein. "Irving," I said, "you're supposed to be a great manager, so explain something to me. Last year Peter Frampton made fifty-two million dollars. Now I'm nearly four times older than he is, and last year I didn't even make fifty-one million dollars." He hung up on me.

I've got to confess this was all a little upsetting, because I had made an album, too. My sister Goldie bought it. But this album goes back a lot of years. I did it for Victor Records. Remember His Master's Voice, with a dog sitting under the phonograph horn? Well, while I was recording, when I got to the second chorus the dog bit me. And on the flip side of the record there was an apology by Thomas Edison.

But getting back to Peter Frampton, let's say he paid his manager 25 percent of his earnings. That means that year his manager made $13 million. Now Al Jolson was the world's greatest entertainer, and Peter Frampton's manager made more money in one year than Jolson made in his lifetime. I heard Frampton's manager sing. The dog would have bitten him, too.

All these rock stars in the cast made fabulous money, and I thought this was why they looked so happy. But it wasn't that at all. I found out it was because some of them smoked grass. Well, I wanted to be happy, too, so one day when nobody was

me her "John Travolta" and I gave her my "Marie Dressler."

Oh, I just remembered something that happened while making the movie that should go in this book. There was a dramatic scene near the end of the picture where Burl Ives rushes across the lawn and gives me a big hug. It's very emotional. Well, we did the scene, but Leonard Stern, our director, didn't like it. He said, "Burl, this is the way I want it done," and he ran across the lawn and hugged me. Then Burl hugged me again, but Leonard still wasn't satisfied. He said, "No, no, like this," and hugged me again. I must confess I enjoyed Leonard's hug more than I did Burl's. In fact, the next day I sent him flowers. I told you it was a very friendly group.

Leonard Stern was a delight to work with. He was creative, considerate, and open to suggestions from everybody. And I'm not saying this because he always photographed me from my best side.

Now at the finish of shooting a movie it's customary to have a wrap party, where everybody involved with the picture gets together one last time before they go their separate ways. While our party was sentimental, it was also a lot of fun. We sang, we danced, we ate, Leonard hugged me again, and Burl Ives got jealous. I gave Brooke Shields a farewell gift of a gold charm bracelet, and she gave me a pair of roller skates. How she knew I needed another pair of roller skates, I'll never know. For me this party was a perfect way to end a wonderful experience.

Now my next movie will be filmed in New York, and— Wait, wait, wait, I just realized I mentioned everybody in *Just You and Me, Kid* except the producers, Jerry Zeitman and Irving Fein. So I better mention them: Jerry Zeitman and Irving Fein. I feel so bad about forgetting them that I'll mention them again: Jerry Zeitman and Irving Fein.

I started to tell you about my newest picture for Warner Brothers. Well, it takes place in New York, and it's about three old guys living on social security. It's called *Going in Style*. By the time you read this it might not be called *Going in Style*, it might be called something else. It might not even take place in New York. In fact, I might not be in the movie. But who cares, as long as I get paid. That's not true; I did make the movie, and it will be shot in New York. You know me, money means nothing. If a director hugs me, I'll work my heart out for him.

This picture stars Art Carney, Lee Strasberg, and myself. We live our dull lives together, sort of waiting out our last years. It's not a musical. And it was a challenge for me because I had to play an old man. I had to learn how to walk slow, how to drop food on my tie, how to remember to forget things, and I had to get to the studio an hour early every morning. It took time for the makeup man to put on wrinkles. You see, I haven't got any wrinkles on the outside, all my wrinkles are on the inside. If any of you would like to buy some inside wrinkles, I'll give them to you wholesale.

I'm really looking forward to making this picture. It's a fine script, and very exciting, too. These three old guys aren't just sitting around, they're up to something . . . which I could tell you, but won't. I want my book to have a little suspense, too. The script was written by a young new talent, Martin Brest, who's also directing. I can tell you one thing, this kid is a perfectionist. He called me up one day and said, "Mr. Burns, I want you to wear different glasses in this movie. Can I stop by and have you try on a few pair?"

"Sure, why not."

Well, he came in on a Thursday with a photographer, a lighting man, three suitcases full of eyeglasses, and a consulting optometrist. They set up the lights, I put on glasses, I took off glasses, and they kept taking pictures. Well, it didn't take long; by the following Wednesday Martin was satisfied. Then he decided that I would need a different hair style. He wanted me to look like somebody else. That seemed strange, if he wanted me to look like somebody else, why didn't he hire somebody else? But I guess that's show business. When he asked me to go to the wig-maker I told him I'd be glad to but he'd have to wait for a few days until my eyes got back in focus.

But when it was all over, I did look entirely different. With my new hair, my new glasses, my new wrinkles, and walking with the spots on my tie, I looked so different that when I called up my manager Irving Fein, he didn't hang up on me.

As soon as I'm finished with this movie I'll be playing myself again, I'll be doing a sequel to *Oh God!* Now I'm sure some of you are wondering why God would come down a second time. Well, there's a very good reason. The first time He came down He made the studio $65 million. Who knows, if the box office holds up, I might come down another seven or eight times. This could turn out to be bigger than *Charlie Chan*.

Well, that about brings you up to date on my new career. I've made five pictures and have one coming up. There's one very important thing I've learned about acting, and I'd like to pass it on to any young aspiring actor who might be reading this. And remember this for the rest of your life: To be a fine actor, when you're playing a role you've got to be honest. And if you can fake that, you've got it made.

W. CHARLES EMORY DID IT THE HARD WAY

ALL WRITERS HAVE their own way of working. Take Ernest Hemingway, he did all his writing standing up at his typewriter. I tried that, but I couldn't type standing up . . . and I couldn't type sitting down . . . I can't type.

Now F. Scott Fitzgerald did his best work while he was drinking. So I tried that, too. I fixed a martini, but nothing came to me, so I fixed myself another one. Then after the fourth martini I started writing. Well, I kept writing and drinking, and drinking and writing, and when I woke up the next afternoon I couldn't wait to see some of the great stuff I had written. But there was one thing wrong with it: I could read it but I couldn't understand it.

I also heard that W. Charles Emory locked himself in his bedroom naked to do his writing. I didn't even try that. If I'm naked in a bedroom, I'm not writing.

So I finally developed my own method. I don't write a book, I talk it. At first I talked into a tape recorder, but there was no reaction. I was telling all these funny anecdotes and wasn't getting any laughs. It threw my timing off. So I got rid of the tape recorder and started interviewing writers. The one who laughed the loudest got the job.

When I started this book I only had one writer, Elon Packard, who had been with me fourteen years, and Jack Langdon, my secretary, who's been with me for nineteen. Jack doesn't type very well, screws up all my appointments, and he can't make a good cup of coffee. Now this isn't going to hurt his feelings because he can't read either. But he's got one admirable quality that makes him indispensable to me: he knows just when I need a laugh.

But there was one day when there was nothing to laugh about. Jack and I came to work one morning as usual, but Packy never showed up. A little later we learned that he had died in his sleep the night before. It was a terrible shock and I felt awful. In fact, for some time I couldn't bring myself to work on the book. But what can you do about those things. We all have to make the same exit. Like in the early days of vaudeville, if the manager didn't like your act, he'd give you back your pictures and that meant you were canceled. Packy got back his pictures. Eventually I'll get mine.

Around this same time I was signed to do a TV special for CBS, so I brought in four writers to work on it. They not only could write, but more important, they were very loud laughers. In fact, they were so good that after the special I signed them to laugh through this book with me. You see, it doesn't matter to me how many writers I have writing this book, I might have thousands before I'm through. That way I don't have to worry about the public. If each writer buys a copy, I've got a best seller. Imagine Hemingway standing there writing a book all by himself. What a dumb businessman.

Actually, I have always believed in giving credit where credit is due. From page 59 on this book has been written with the considerable help of the team of Fred Fox and Seaman Jacobs. Each of them has a nice sense of humor and is a very clever writer. And then there's Hal Goldman. He has a nice sense of humor and is a very clever writer. The fourth is Lisa Miller. She has a nice sense of humor and is a very clever writer.

You'll notice that in the above paragraph I said the same thing about each of them. Well, I'm not stupid; the four of them are sitting right here in the room with me. The truth is we all get along fine. No one worries about who says what. There's no credit, and no blame. Five mornings a week I meet with them for exactly two hours. This is enough time to accomplish something, but not enough for us to get sick of each other. When the two hours are up, that's it. They can go about their business, and I can go roller skating. It's a very pleasant arrangement. We have lots of laughs, and I enjoy working with them. And I think Seaman, Fred, Hal and Lisa enjoy working with me. Why shouldn't they? After all, I have a nice sense of humor and I'm a very clever writer—I mean, a very clever talker!

IF THIS WERE A SERIOUS BOOK, THIS WOULD BE THE LAST CHAPTER

WELL, YOU'VE COME a long way with me. The Peewee Quartet wasn't yesterday. Looking back over all those years since then, there were ups and downs, and some tears, but there were also lots of laughs, lots of love, lots of wonderful memories, and it was never boring. If you can think of anything better, let me know. But hurry.

My friends keep telling me I've mellowed, that things don't upset me like they used to ten or twenty years ago. That's what they tell me, and I'm convinced. Now if they can just convince the guys I play bridge with. But it's true, people do change. Each day you're a different person. Who knows, tomorrow I may be Cary Grant or Robert Redford. That wouldn't bother me too much as long as I could stay in show business.

I'm constantly asked which I preferred, vaudeville, radio, television, or movies. I could never answer that because I'm nuts about all of them. Of course, when you analyze it, each medium had its advantages. That was even true with silent pictures. John Gilbert, one of silent pictures' biggest stars, sounded like a chicken when he talked. Radio was just the opposite. In radio the voice was all that counted. It didn't matter what you looked

like. If they'd ever had a thing called silent radio, my brother
Sammy would have been a smash.

As I said, if it's show business, I love it. And I love it as
much today as when I first went into it. In fact, I can hardly
wait for vaudeville to come back. I saved all my funny hats. But
I don't think show business has changed that much. At least
comedy hasn't. There may be variations in style and techniques,
but if a joke is basically funny, it lives forever. And it's the same
today as it was for Smith and Dale; if the audience laughs,
you're a hit, and if they don't laugh, you can always take up
singing like I did.

To me it's as simple as that. You do the best you can, and
you don't overanalyze, because things rarely work out the way
you would expect. Take these movies I've been doing lately.
Each time they put me with a younger co-star. First it was
Walter Matthau in *The Sunshine Boys*. Then in *Oh God!* I played
opposite John Denver. In *Just You and Me, Kid* it was fourteen-
year-old Brooke Shields, and in the sequel to *Oh God!* my co-star
will be a girl who's eleven years old. I don't know who they have
in mind for me after that, but I'm not taking any chances; I'm
learning how to change a diaper.

But I'm not complaining, because I really get a kick out of
working with young people. I've never understood all this talk
about the generation gap. I never knew what that meant. I guess
it was the way I was brought up. There were fifteen of us
crowded into three rooms; my grandmother, my mother and
father, and seven sisters and five brothers, all different ages.
And we got along just fine. There was no gap, we didn't have
room for one. We were lucky to have room for my grandmother.

I do think young people are great. I've always enjoyed their
company. Now that doesn't mean you can turn back the clock. I
see some older people try that, with the medallions and the tight
jeans, and it can get pretty ridiculous. I've never lied about my
age. If you're going to lie, lie about something important; like

telling your wife there's no other woman; or telling the other woman you don't have a wife.

In our youth-oriented society we tend to forget the advantages of my present stage of life. Now that I've seen eighty-three summers come and go, let me leave you with a few thoughts on a subject I know something about:

I've been young and I've been old, but I never knew when young ended and old began. . . .

Old people are healthier than a lot of young people who died with the same ailment *they* have. . . .

Just because you're old that doesn't mean you're more forgetful. The same people whose names I can't remember now I couldn't remember fifty years ago. . . .

They say you can't teach an old dog new tricks. Who needs new tricks? If you play it right, the old tricks still work. . . .

Walter Matthau once asked me, "George, when did sex stop for you?" I told him, "At two o'clock this morning." . . .

I enjoy being old. For one thing, I'm still here. I like being older than I was yesterday. And I'm looking forward to being older tomorrow than I am today. When you're young, if you're lucky, you get older. When you're middle-aged, if you're lucky you'll get to be old. But when you're old, you're in a holding pattern—that's it. It's sort of a reward for being young all that time.

WARM LEFTOVERS

For an author my sense of continuity is really pathetic. Here I thought I had finished my book, and I didn't include some of my favorite anecdotes. They don't belong back here, so put them anywhere you want . . . but don't shock me.

Al Jolson used to bill himself AL JOLSON, THE WORLD'S GREATEST ENTERTAINER. Can you imagine anyone billing himself like that and walking out on the stage and having to live up to it? Well, he did. He was the greatest. He might not have been the greatest talent, but he was the greatest entertainer. And he also had the greatest ego. When he was in his dressing room and another act was on the stage performing, Jolson always had the water running. He couldn't stand hearing any other act get applause. When I started in the business that couldn't have happened to me. The dressing room they gave me had no running water.

Now even though Jolson was the greatest and went from one hit show to another, there came a time in his life when there was a lull. He certainly wasn't starving, he always had millions, but the jobs he was offered weren't worthy of "The World's

Greatest Entertainer." During that time sturgeon, which is a very expensive fish, wasn't sold in California, but Jolson was very fond of this delicacy. So every week he used to fly in $150 worth of sturgeon and kept it in the refrigerator at the Hillcrest Country Club. I had lunch with him practically every day, and one day I paid him this tremendous compliment. I said, "Joley, to me you'll always be the greatest showman who ever lived. There will never be anything like you."

He was all smiles, and said, "Thanks, George, and how would you like a little sturgeon for lunch?"

"Sturgeon?" I said, "I'd love it." And it was absolutely delicious. After that every time I saw Jolson I paid him a compliment and I had sturgeon for lunch. It got to the point where I liked sturgeon even more than I did Jolson.

Then Columbia Pictures made *The Jolson Story*. Larry Parks played Jolson, but he didn't do the singing, Jolson did. He sang all the songs on the sound track, and it was the first time in movie history that a sound track was the star of a movie. I saw the film and was thrilled. The next day when I saw Jolson, I said, "Joley, I saw the movie, and that sound track is the greatest thing I've ever heard in my life."

He looked straight at me. "You can buy your own sturgeon, kid, I'm a hit again."

While I'm on Jolson let me tell you one more story. When his career first started taking off he sent his father to Miami for a vacation. Now his father was a very frugal, conservative man. There was a cold spell in Florida that year, so Joley sent his father a camel's hair coat that cost ninety dollars. Well, he couldn't tell the old man how much the coat cost because Joley knew his father would think it was too extravagant. So he called him on the phone and told him he was sending him a coat that cost twenty dollars, to wear it, keep warm, and have a nice vacation. Two days later his father phoned Joley and said, "Joley, send me ten more coats, I just sold this one for thirty-five dollars."

Eddie Cantor was also one of the show business giants. I'd like to do about a minute and a half of Cantor stories, if you read fast. When Eddie was doing his radio show he had four very good writers working for him. One afternoon there was a conflict about a certain joke. Eddie didn't think it was funny, but one of the writers thought it was. So in his very high voice, Eddie said, "Boys, there's a difference of opinion here. But you know me, I'm a very fair man, we'll vote on it."

Well, the four writers voted in favor of the joke. Then Eddie said, "That's four votes in favor of the joke, but it's my show and I get five votes. So write another joke, and if I don't like that one, we'll vote again."

Years ago Eddie Cantor and George Jessel were headlining the Palace Theater, and at the finish of the show they did a routine together. Well, one night Cantor ad-libbed a line that got a big laugh. Then Jessel topped him with an even bigger laugh. Cantor couldn't think of anything to say, so he took his shoe off and hit Jessel over the head with it, and that got a still bigger laugh.

But this really upset Jessel. He walked down to the footlights, and in a grand manner said, "Ladies and gentlemen. This so-called grown-up man, whom I have the misfortune to be working with, is so lacking in decorum, breeding and intelligence, that when he was unable to think of a clever retort he had to resort to the lowest form of cheap slapstick humor by taking off his shoe and striking me on the head. Only an insensitive oaf would stoop so low."

Cantor said, "Georgie, are you through?" Jessel said, "Yes," and with that Cantor hit him on the head with his shoe again, and that brought down the house. This proves one thing; you don't need an education, just get yourself a pair of funny shoes.

On the Eddie Cantor radio shows every week he used big guest stars. If he had a funny joke, it went into the show. It didn't matter who did it. He would give the same joke to Gracie, Gregory Peck, or even the Mad Russian.

I'll never forget one time Jack Benny was the guest star, and when Jack came to rehearsal he learned that the script called for him to play the cello. Jack couldn't believe it. "Eddie," he said, "how come you've got me playing the cello? For fifty years I've been playing the violin."

"But, Jack," Eddie said, "it's funny. Let's take a vote."

"Oh no, I know how you vote," Jack said. "You leave me with the writers and let me work on it." And Cantor did. Jack and the writers rewrote the script where Jack played the violin, and it was a big hit. But Cantor didn't waste anything. On his show three weeks later he had Charles Boyer playing the cello.

Jack Benny was a tremendous star for the last fifty years of his life. Big things like million-dollar contracts, changing networks, staying in the Top Ten, these big decisions he could handle. It was the little day-to-day things that threw him. The smaller they were, the bigger the problem for Jack. There was the time he and I were having lunch at the Brown Derby, and he couldn't decide whether or not to put butter on his bread. He said, "You know, I hate bread without butter."

"Well, put butter on it then," I said.

"I can't," he sighed. "Mary put me on a diet and she said no butter."

"Then eat it without butter."

"But I love butter. Bread is nothing without butter."

"So put butter on it."

"I better call Mary."

"Jack, please, make this one decision yourself!"

Well, he had butter, and when the check came for the lunch, I said, "Give it to Jack Benny."

"Why should I pay the check?" Jack asked.

"Because," I said, "if you don't, I'll tell Mary you had butter."

* * *

Another story about Jack was when Mary, Gracie, Jack, and I went to Honolulu for a vacation. The girls flew over, and Jack and I sailed on the S.S. *Lurline*. We thought we'd have a few days' rest. Now on the *Lurline* everybody dressed for dinner, so on the first night we were in our suite getting dressed, and Jack put on a yellow dinner jacket. "What do you think of this jacket?" he asked me.

"It's beautiful," I said.

"Mary doesn't like it."

I said, "Well, Mary's not wearing it."

Shaking his head, Jack said, "I can't understand it, why doesn't Mary like it?"

How was I supposed to know? Maybe it reminded her of butter. "Jack," I said, "you look darling in that jacket."

"Good," he said happily, "I'll wear it tonight and enjoy it."

"Of course," I muttered.

Then admiring himself in the mirror, Jack said, "I can't figure Mary out, what's wrong with it?"

"There's nothing wrong with it. C'mon, let's go to dinner."

"Maybe I should wear something else. What do you think?"

"I don't care what the hell you wear," I said, a little exasperated. "Let's go to dinner."

"George, take a good look at it, front and back." As he turned around I said, "I'll see you in the dining room," and left. Ten minutes later in came Jack wearing his blue dinner jacket. I never mentioned it all during dinner. The next night out came the yellow dinner jacket again. "George," he said, "I'm going to wear it tonight." I never answered him. He looked at himself in the mirror and said, "I think it looks great." I didn't even look at him. "Mary wears a lot of things I don't like," he went on, "and I don't tell her what to wear. . . . If Mary knew I was wearing this tonight, she'd kill me. . . . It drives me nuts, I don't know why she doesn't like it! I'm not a fool, I'm over twenty-one and I know what looks good on me! And this jacket happens to look great on me!"

While he was still talking I went up to dinner. I had a cocktail, finished my soup, and was in the middle of my entree, when in came my roommate from Waukegan wearing his blue dinner jacket. Every night it was the same routine: "Should I wear it? . . . Shouldn't I wear it? . . . Mary doesn't like it . . . But I like it! . . ." but the yellow jacket never made it to dinner.

Finally the last night out we were ready to go to dinner, and Jack was wearing his blue dinner jacket. I said, "Jack, you love that yellow dinner jacket but you haven't worn it once. Tonight is your last chance. Wear it! I'll take an oath that I won't tell Mary."

Just a bit annoyed, Jack said, "Look, I'm not afraid of Mary."

"Then why aren't you wearing it?"

"I'm saving it on purpose," he snapped. "I'm going to wear it when the four of us go out to dinner in Hawaii to prove to you that I'm not afraid of Mary."

Well, we had dinner, and the next day as we were getting off the boat, Jimmy, our steward, came up to Jack and said, "Mr. Benny, I want to thank you again for giving me that nice yellow dinner jacket." Jack never looked at me, he just kept walking.

"Jimmy," I said.

"Yes, Mr. Burns?"

"Don't ever wear that jacket in front of Mary Benny."

It seems as though I've known George Jessel all my life, but back in the twenties when I first met him he was starring in *The Jazz Singer* on Broadway. And Jessel was really a great actor. I saw the show one night and it affected me very deeply. The story was about the son of a Jewish cantor who goes into show business against his father's wishes. Just before the High Holidays the father dies, and the son gives up show business, comes into the synagogue, and takes his father's place. At the finish of the play he sings "Kol Nidre," the holiest of all Hebrew melodies. Well, when the curtain came down I was a wreck, I was crying like a baby. I felt I had seen my own life, because my father was a cantor. I ran backstage to congratulate Jessel on his marvelous performance, but Jessel's manager was standing at the dressing room door and told me I couldn't go in. "Why not?" I asked. "I want to tell him how much I enjoyed his performance."

He said, "I'm sorry, you can't go in, he's in there naked."

"So what?" I said. "I've seen a naked Jew before. I want to tell him how great he was."

"Mr. Burns," he insisted, "he's got a girl in there."

So I left. I was really shocked. I didn't think anything could follow "Kol Nidre."

Throughout George Jessel's life he always seemed to be involved in some emotional crisis. I'll never forget when he was married to Norma Talmadge and she left him. He learned that she was going around with some doctor in Florida and this really set him off. He bought a gun and chartered an open-cockpit plane and flew directly to Florida. He went straight to her hotel, knocked on the door, and when she opened it there was this doctor. Jessel pulled out his gun and took a shot at him. However, he missed the doctor, the bullet went through the window and hit a gardener two blocks away who was bent over picking up a daisy.

Well, the gardener took Jessel to court. The judge asked, "Mr. Jessel, how is it possible for you to take a shot at someone ten feet away from you and hit a gardener two blocks away?"

Jessel answered, "Your Honor, I'm an actor, not Buffalo Bill!"

I've mentioned my personal manager, Irving Fein, several

times in this book, and aside from hanging up the phone, he has other talents. I'm glad to say that if it weren't for Irving, I wouldn't have this new movie career. In fact, he keeps me so busy I hardly have time to talk about him. He's honest, enthusiastic, fearless, full of ideas, and a great businessman. So much for the compliments. Now let me tell you about the real Irving Fein.

I found out that if it concerns me, there's no problem, nothing is difficult. I'm eighty-three years old, and he has me running around like I'm just starting in show business. One morning he came bouncing into the office all smiles and said, "George, we're going to do another TV special for CBS."

I said, "Oh, are we? Good, then you can do those same songs and dances that you did in the last special."

Irving gave me a courtesy laugh and continued. "George, this will be a breeze. We'll have some kind of a big opening, then the orchestra will play 'Ain't Misbehavin',' then you'll come out and do five minutes of funny stuff . . . you know, great topical jokes or whatever, and then you sing two or three songs. So far it's easy, right?"

I didn't say anything, so he took another breath and continued. "Then you introduce your first guest star and let them do their own bit. Maybe then you do sort of a five-minute hunk with them . . . no, I'll make it even easier for you, just do four minutes. Then you do some show business stories which are always good for twenty or thirty big laughs, go into your sand dance, and before you know it we're up to the middle commercial."

I just sat there dying to learn how easy the second half was going to be. I didn't have to wait long.

"The second half," Irving went on, "we open with something different, something that's never been done before, something that people don't expect from you. Right there we've got a good five minutes. Then we go into a production number with about eight or ten girls . . . you don't have to bother with that, but it would be better if you came in for the finish. But anyway, you do a few more songs, a few more sketches, bring on a couple more guest stars, then do a dramatic finish, and we've got our show."

I kept smoking my cigar and looking at him. Then very quietly I said, "Irving, it can't miss, that show is bound to win an Emmy."

He said, "All we've got left to do is come up with a clever title, like . . . like . . . uh . . . you know, it's easy . . . something clever."

"Irving," I said, "you've got it worked out so well I won't even have to hire writers."

"And, George, the best part is," he stated, "you've got ten weeks to prepare the special. While you're doing that you can finish your movie."

"How can I do a movie and prepare a special at the same time?" I inquired.

"George," he assured me, "they're both in Los Angeles."

"Well, now I feel better," I said. Then I added, "Irving, I might have one Sunday off, maybe you can book me for a concert."

Irving just smiled. "George," he said, "I know you're putting me on, but I forgot to tell you the best part. When you're doing the special you don't have to use makeup."

Now that's how Irving Fein operates—almost. I did do the special, I did do the movie, but I broke Irving's heart. I didn't do the Sunday concert.

There's a footnote to this story. As we finished writing this Irving happened to walk in the room, so we read it to him. I said, "Irving, if there's anything you don't like, we'll take it out."

He said, "No, no, it makes me look like a dope, but leave it in. It's more important that you finish the book, because we're leaving for London in two weeks to play the Palladium."

*   *   *

When I was about twenty-four or twenty-five and a small-time vaudeville actor, I used to hang out at a little restaurant called Wiennig and Sberber on Forty-fifth Street in New York. In those days one could get a full course dinner for thirty-five cents. When I wasn't working they would let me sign for the meal. I'd run up a bill for four or five dollars, and when I'd get a job I'd pay them. One time I owed them $163, which gives you an idea of how well I was doing.

Wiennig's was a popular hangout for actors, newspaper people, politicians, prizefighters, song pluggers and, late at night, prostitutes. Some of them were very pretty, but it turned out they didn't give credit like Wiennig.

Let me tell you something about the partners who owned this restaurant. They were a couple of real characters. Sberber had a habit of smelling anything before he bought it. This habit started out with cigars but it spread to everything else. One time a man came in to sell him napkins, Sberber put one to his nose, sniffed it, and said, "I'll take six dozen." Another time a chair collapsed under a customer sitting at my table. Sberber rushed over to help him up, and I said, "Sberber, you got a bad chair there. Didn't you smell it before you bought it?"

Sberber never stopped talking, but nobody ever knew what he was talking about. Harry Richman came in there one night for a late supper, and Sberber tried to impress him. He came up to the table and said, "Mr. Richman, thanks for coming in. It's a pleasure to see such a talent eating here. From the way you sing I can tell you must like music."

Richman didn't want to encourage the conversation, so he just said, "Thank you."

Sberber said, "I like music, too."

"You do?" Richman muttered.

"Do I like music?" Sberber went on, "I come from Chicago." While Richman was trying to figure that out Sberber said, "My daughter is even taking singing lessons. You'll never guess from who."

Making up a name, Richman asked, "It couldn't be Teresa La Guardia?"

Sberber said, "It couldn't, huh? She charges fifteen dollars a lesson."

By now Richman was eating very fast. Sberber said, "I love good music. I'm always at the opera. I've seen *Carmen* seventeen times, I know it by heart."

Richman couldn't resist this. He turned to Sberber and said, "You know *Carmen* by heart? How does it go?"

Sberber said, "Good."

And that was Sberber. Now let me tell you a little about Wiennig. He was a different type of character. He was the kind who only remembered his last conversation. If you asked him a question, he gave you the answer to the last customer's question. One night I came in and said to him, "Have you seen Manny Mannishaw?"

Wiennig said, "Look on the floor, maybe it fell down."

Another time I asked, "Wiennig, did I get any phone calls?"

His answer was, "How do you like that? You give a waiter a chance to go up and he goes down."

He never called the customers by their names. Al Jolson would come in, and Wiennig would say, "'April Showers,' would you like table two?" With Sophie Tucker he'd holler out, "Waiter, make room for 'Some of These Days'!" Me, he called "Lay Off." I don't know why he was upset, I only owed him $163.

When the restaurant was crowded Wiennig would help by waiting on the tables. Once while he was doing that a customer stopped him and asked, "Where's the men's room?"

Wiennig said, "Please, I've only got two hands!"

Well, I had a lot of happy times there, and it was a big kick for me to see all those big personalities who came. But the biggest kick was knowing Wiennig and Sberber. I wonder if Sberber smelled Wiennig before he made him a partner.

ROASTED, TOASTED, AND FRIED

THROUGHOUT MY BOOK I talked and talked and talked about myself. Now that you know what I think about me, maybe we should wind up this whole thing with a few honest opinions. I was the Guest of Honor on one of the Dean Martin Television Roasts, and this is what some of my lovable colleagues said about me. Now being honored at one of these roasts is a lot like the way General Custer was honored by the Indians at Little Big Horn. The only difference was I knew what was coming; a lot of age jokes . . . going out with young girls . . . my singing . . . my sex life . . . my toupee . . . and they didn't disappoint me.

Here are a few excerpts from their remarks, starting with the host of this unforgettable occasion:

Dean Martin

"Tonight we salute our Man of the Hour, George Burns. We are honoring George tonight by special request—*his*. . . .
Though George is recognized as one of our truly great comedians, he'd rather be recognized for his singing. The fact is he started out as a singer. I don't want to say *when* he started

singing, but that was the year the Top Ten were the Ten Commandments! . . .

Did you ever hear a voice like his? He sings like he makes love—a slow start and no finish! . . .

Funny thing, but women are always fascinated by George. Even when George was a kid he had a lot of charisma. Then he started dating girls, and his charisma cleared up!

(So far I was right, the jokes were about my age, my singing, and my sex life. Dean's wrong about that charisma, that didn't clear up until I was thirty-eight.)

Milton Berle

"Ladies and gentlemen, it's a great thrill to be here tonight to honor George Burns! *Yes, it's a great thrill!!* I'm speaking loud so he can hear me. . . .

Look at him sitting there. He doesn't know this is a Roast. He thinks he's having sex. . . .

This man's back goes out more than he does. . . . It's the truth. The other day I gave him a copy of *The Joy of Sex*. He took out his crayons and colored it. . . .

Boy, what a beautiful life George Burns is leading right now. Luncheon every day at the Polo Lounge in Beverly Hills— dinner every night with a gorgeous young chick—he's already won an Oscar—he's written a best-selling book—and gets offers from every movie studio in town. Oh God . . . I can't wait until I get old! . . ."

(Being a good straight man I sat there and laughed at all the right spots. But after the roast I told Milton I loved his joke about my back going out more than I do. And I asked him if I could use it. Milton said, "Why not, I stole it from you.")

Gene Kelly

"It's a great pleasure to be here to honor my old friend George Burns. Now I'm expected to say some awful things about him. But not me. After seeing some of the things he did in his movie *Oh God!* he might make it rain in my living room. . . . A little while back George was doing a television special and he asked me to be one of his guests. He wanted me to recreate a scene I did in the movie *An American In Paris*. That's the one where I sang and danced on the banks of the Seine with Leslie Caron. Well, I thought it was a marvelous idea and was all for it until George suggested that instead of doing a romantic Gershwin song he wanted me to sing one of *his* songs, 'The Monkey Rag.' . . . I told him if I had sung 'The Monkey Rag' to Leslie Caron in the picture, she would have thrown me right into the Seine. George told me not to worry, Leslie Caron wasn't on the show and I was going to sing it to Phyllis Diller. So I had no argument. 'The Monkey Rag' is a perfect song for Phyllis Diller. . . . George, I loved you in *The Sunshine Boys*, I loved you in *Oh God!*, and I even love you in between pictures."

(I love Gene as much as he loves me, but it never would have worked out. Eventually he would have found out I was Jewish.)

Red Buttons

"Ladies and gentlemen, the question tonight is why, why are we toasting this ancient comedian . . . a man old enough to be his own father. . . . A man who embarrassed everybody at The Last Supper by asking for seconds. . . . A man, who, when Rome was burning, requested Nero to play 'You Picked a Fine Time to Leave Me, Lucille'. . . . And this is the type of person we're honoring tonight? . . .

And thank you, George Burns, for just being you. I love
you!"

> (How fickle can you be? First he chops me to pieces,
> then he tells me he loves me. I like Red Buttons, he's
> a nice kid, but I'm not cheating on Gene Kelly.)

Tom Dreesen

"You know, you just can't imagine how it is for me, a new
performer, to be on the same dais with all these famous stars.
And it's especially exciting that the Guest of Honor is George
Burns, who's been my idol since I was a child . . . since my
mother was a child . . . since my grandmother was a child
. . . since my great grandmother was a child. . . . Look, I'll
keep going until I get a laugh. . . .
In closing, I want you to know that when I started out in
show business, an old vaudevillian pulled me aside and said,
'Would you like to become a good comedian?' I said, 'Yes,'
and he said, 'Well, study the masters. Watch George Burns.
In fact, watch his every move.' Mr. Burns, I've been watching
you all night long . . . you haven't moved once!"

> (It's always a pleasure to watch a young comedian work.
> And I'm very happy when I see one of them make it big.
> It's when more than one makes it that I start
> to get a little nervous.)

Jimmy Stewart

"George Burns and I go back together a long while. We were
both at the MGM studio at the same time . . . 1938. In those
days I was a romantic juvenile and George was an old
man. . . . And it's just amazing that now, forty years later,
we're both still at it. Only now *I'm* the old man, and George is
the romantic juvenile. . . ."

(I love to watch Jimmy work. He takes his time . . . he
stutters . . . and he stammers . . . he puckers his lips . . .
he drawls . . . he swallows and he gulps . . . he's amazing.
He gets more laughs not saying anything than most
comedians get saying it. . . . Even when he's not working
he talks slow, and he walks slow, and he eats slow. I asked
his wife Gloria, "Does Jimmy do everything slow?" She
paused and said, "I'm trying to remember.")

Ruth Buzzi

(Playing the old spinster, "Gladys Ormphby")
"Tonight, ladies and gentlemen, you're in for a surprise.
George Burns, the man you see sitting there, he and I used to
go around together. And let me tell you something, George
was not the greatest lover in the world. In fact, he had a mean
streak in him. Most men will cover your face with kisses. He
covered mine with a burlap bag. . . .
George Burns wasn't the same person you see today. He
didn't even like the smell of those big, fat cigars. So I stopped
smoking them. . . . We were poor in those days. We had no
car, but George had a bicycle to take him to auditions. He
used to let me ride in the basket of his bike. That's how I got
my nickname . . . Old Waffle-Bottom! . . ."

(You know, Ruth Buzzi is a very pretty girl. It must take a
lot of effort and hard work for her to make herself
look so unattractive. I know, because I have to work
just as hard not to look the way I look.)

Abe Vigoda

"I suppose I should say it's a great pleasure to be here tonight,
but it would be a lie. I'm an old, tired man, and I should be
home in bed—alone. . . .
In all the years I've been watching television, not once was I
able to stay up for the *Late Show* . . . Recently I've been falling

asleep during the *Early Show*. . . . Last week I could hardly
make it through *News at Noon*. . . ."

**(I was the Guest of Honor, he spoke for seven minutes and
never even mentioned my name. That was the nicest thing
that was said about me all night.)**

Dom De Luise

(Playing the part of a psychiatrist)
"George Burns came to me, because after playing 'God,' he
thought he was. So I put him on the couch and said, 'Mr.
Burns, you came to the right doctor. I can cure anybody. I
once cured a man who thought he was a rabbit. Of course, I
must admit not before he and his wife had seventy-eight
children.' . . .
And just to humor George, I said, 'I hope you don't make it
rain again for forty days and forty nights.' What do you think
he said? He said, 'If I do, you better build yourself an ark and
fill it with pairs—with a pair of elephants . . . a pair of tigers
. . . a pair of horses . . . Raquel Welch'. . . ."

**(I've got to correct Dom's last remark. I never said
that. I never even mentioned Raquel Welch. I said Dolly
Parton. If you're going to do jokes like that,
why not be subtle?)**

Phyllis Diller

"You know, Dean Martin does know how to relax. It takes
him an hour and a half to watch *Sixty Minutes*. . . .
You don't know what a thrill this is for me to be here with
George Burns. I've had a crush on George for years. He's my
kind of guy. He's handsome . . . he's successful . . . and he's
breathing. . . .
I don't know how you feel about old age, George, but in my
case I didn't even see it coming. It hit me from the rear. . . .

But, George, I just want to tell you this. After the show—I know it's your night, but I'd love to share it with you—somehow . . . we'll find a way. Come to my room if you want to see a real woman—I'll get one for you!"

(Phyllis Diller is a great comedienne, and she's always putting herself down. But don't believe it. She's a very charming lady. And about her saying that she liked me because I'm handsome, successful, and breathing, every time I meet her to make that joke believable I start to breathe.)

Frank Welker

(The Impressionist)

"Good evening, everyone, this is Walter Cronkite. Tonight we pay homage to a man who is celebrating his seventy-fifth anniversary in show business. George owes much to the miracles of modern medicine—just how much only Medicare knows for sure. . . . But through the miracles of modern medicine George Burns still chases pretty girls, and through the miracle of modern psychiatry he intends to find out why. . . . You see, when you're his age, the memory is the second thing to go. . . .

Good night, George. This is Walter Cronkite signing off with the words I told my wife on our wedding night, so many, many years ago: 'That's the way it is.'"

(Frank Welker is a very talented young mimic. He not only does Walter Cronkite, he does everybody. He does me so well that one night I got confused and thought I was Frank Welker. I took this girl to dinner and then we went to my place. We had a couple of drinks, and at ten o'clock I suddenly found out I was George Burns and sent her home.)

Jack Carter

"I'm delighted to be here for my dear, sweet friend George
Burns. What an adorable man. The sweetheart of the Stone
Age. . . . This wonderful Neil Sedaka reject singer. . . . This
beautiful man who was the first performer to give a one-man
concert at Carnegie Hall. Fortunately, the next night two men
showed up! . . ."

(Jack, I hope you won't be upset because I didn't use any
more of your stuff. But some of it was too risqué, some of
it was too political, and let's face it, nine-tenths
of it was just too funny.)

Connie Stevens

"I had a marvelous time last night, and who do you think was
my date—George Burns. I picked him up right after his
nap. . . . It was then that I discovered George's secret for
staying young. He never overextends himself. He wouldn't
even whistle for a cab. He figures when he finally gets up a
pucker, why waste it on a taxi. . . . We were driving along
and all of a sudden George leaned over and said, 'My leg's
asleep. It's numb. I can't feel a thing.' I said, 'George, please
relax . . . that's my knee you're holding.' . . . Anyway, when
the evening was over he took me to my room and kissed me
good night. Can I tell you something. It was a pretty hot
kiss—he forgot to take the cigar out of his mouth. . . ."

(I love Connie. We did a television show together called
Wendy and Me. It was really a good show. And Connie was
a delight to work with. She was never late for rehearsals—
except once. The morning after she got married
she was ten minutes late.)

Orson Welles

"As for our honored guest, George Burns, he certainly deserves more respect than he's been getting here tonight. After all, how many men his age could listen to insults about their sex lives . . . without the use of a hearing aid? . . . All these slurs about George's amorous adventures remind me of the words of the poetess Elizabeth Barrett Browning: 'How do I love thee? Let me count the ways.' In your case, George, don't bother to count the ways, just count the times. . . .
As for you, George, in your long and glorious career you've been the recipient of a perfect plethora of honors and awards. You've triumphed on radio, conquered TV, and headlined at The Palace. You have known presidents and kings. You, more than any living mortal, should be cognizant that there is something more exciting in life than women and sex. And whoever finds out what it is will make a fortune. . . ."

(I love to listen to Orson Welles. That dramatic delivery, the beauty of his voice, his diction, his excellent vocabulary, I sit there spellbound. But the problem is I don't know what the hell he's talking about. I never went to college. I never went to high school. I never got past the fourth grade in grammar school. I was really stupid, and I was very good at it. In fact, in kindergarten I flunked sandbox. I didn't know a teeter from a totter.)

La Wanda Page

"George Burns, honey, you oughta be ashamed of yourself, datin' all them young foxes at your age. A man as old as you, honey, should be *re*-spected, *re*-warded, and *re*-tired—and *re*-treaded. . . .
George, you're too old to get married again. Not only can't you cut the mustard, honey, you're too old to open the jar. . . .

I know what I'm talkin' about, George Burns. I was once married to an old guy myself, honey. When we faced the preacher, he didn't say 'I do'—he said, 'I'll try'. . . ."

(I enjoyed watching LaWanda Page again, she's such a marvelous comedienne. And I want to thank her for saying all those things about me. Compared to what she used to hit Redd Foxx with on *Sanford and Son*, I consider myself complimented.)

Ronald Reagan

"I just couldn't turn down this opportunity to say a few words about our Man of the Hour . . . this Bionic Geriatric . . . this Sun-City Fonzie . . . George Burns . . . the only man I know who does fool Mother Nature. . . .

George, Nancy wanted me to tell you that you're her favorite singer. But then, Harry Truman was her favorite piano player. . . . Just the other night I thought she had one of your records on. It turned out to be a spoon caught in the garbage disposal. . . .

If you're wondering why we're honoring this man tonight, who else do you know who was an actual eyewitness to most of the history of our country? . . . It was George Burns who told Betsy Ross, 'Personally, I feel the pattern's a little busy, but let's run it up the flagpole and see if anyone salutes it.' . . ."

(I've known Ronnie Reagan for a long time. Years ago when he was just getting into show business, every time I met him at a party we'd get up and sing a song together. Since then he became President of the Screen Actors Guild, did a great job as Governor of California, was almost nominated for President of the United States, and still might be. I can't understand it, where did I go wrong. I know I sing better than he does.)

Charlie Callas

"Good evening, my name is Doctor Cooper, George Burns' personal physician. But before I talk about my famous patient, don't forget to buy my book, *Brain Surgery Self-Taught*. . . .

The first time George Burns came to my office he complained about a ringing in his ear. I cured him. I gave him an unlisted ear. . . .

Mr. Burns is always bragging about his sex life. I happen to know he's at the age now when he checks into a motel it's to catch up on his Bible reading. . . . And he has to take somebody with him, those Bibles are heavy. . . ."

(Charlie Callas is a very talented comedian and gets very big laughs. But can I tell you something. I read his book, *Brain Surgery Self-Taught*. Don't try it unless you've got steady hands.)

Don Rickles

"George, we're both of the Jewish world. Not that that matters to show business, but it matters to me. And on behalf of the Jewish religion, we want you out. . . .

Last night George took a girl up to his room here at the hotel. When they left he noticed a sign on the door, 'Have you forgotten anything?' George said, 'Yeah . . . how?' . . .

George, you're beautiful. I'll give you five dollars if you'll marry mother, and thirty dollars if you have a baby. I always wanted a fifty-year-old baby brother. . . ."

**(Don was the last speaker. He's always the last speaker, nobody can follow that guy.
Wait a minute, remember at the beginning of this chapter I said they were all going to do jokes about my age . . . my**

going out with young girls . . . my singing . . . my sex life
. . . and my toupee? The thing I can't get over is that no
one mentioned my toupee. But I think I know the reason. I
turned out to be such a great actor that I've got them all
believing it's my own hair.)

Dean Martin

"Ladies and gentlemen, now we'll hear from our Man of the
Hour, the beautiful George Burns!!
Will somebody help him up!"

George Burns

"Thank you, thank you, ladies and gentlemen. You know,
I've really come a long way in show business. Here I am
eighty-two years old, and to think that all these lovely people
flew all the way to Las Vegas, got all dressed up and came
down here tonight just to insult me. I'm very touched. . . .
Let me tell you something. I was a small-time vaudeville actor
until I was twenty-seven years old, so I'm used to being
insulted. I've been insulted by some of the nicest audiences in
the country. People used to stand in line and pay thirty-five
cents just to come in and insult me. . . . I was insulted at the
Jefferson Theater on Fourteenth Street, at the Gaiety Theater
in Altoona, at the Farley Theater in Brooklyn, at the Colonial
in Akron . . . I can hardly remember a theater I haven't been
insulted in. . . .
Oh, I must tell you what happened at the Farley Theater. I
was in the middle of my act, singing 'In the Heart of a
Cherry,' and just before my yodeling finish the manager
walked out on the stage and canceled me. . . . And to make
matters worse, the audience applauded him. . . . And as he
dragged me off the stage the musicians gave him a standing
ovation. . . .

But nothing fazed me. I got so used to being disliked I thought I was doing well. . . .

When I played in a theater I didn't care if the whole audience hated me. As long as I was on that stage I knew there was one person there who loved me. . . .

So, ladies and gentlemen on the dais, your insults about me tonight meant nothing. I've been insulted by pros. . . . In fact, I played on the bill with Swain's Cats and Rats, and they refused to dress next door to me. . . .

Even when I was working with Gracie I got a notice in Oklahoma City that was a beauty. We were playing the Orpheum Theater and the next morning there was a review in the paper that said, 'Miss Allen is not only a beautiful young lady, but a great talent. Her dancing is exciting and her comedy timing is flawless. There is no telling how far Miss Allen could go if she worked alone'. . . . I saved that review, that was one of the good ones. . . .

But to show you what a nice man I am, I never got cocky. I never allowed these insults to go to my head. Just last year when Frank Sinatra played here in Las Vegas all the women threw their hotel keys up on the stage. The same thing happened to me. When I played Las Vegas women threw their hotel keys at me, too. But it was after they checked out. . . .

So in conclusion, I want to thank all of my friends up here for coming tonight, and I enjoyed the evening very much. You know, right now I'm at a very comfortable stage in my life. I was always taught to respect my elders. Well, I've finally reached the age where I don't have to respect anybody. . . . Thank you."

(Now I've had a few comments about everybody who spoke that night, so I feel I should have something to say about myself.

But I've used up all my good stuff, so this is the end of the book.)